G000075611

COOK'S KITCHEN

Delicious
Cupcakes

igloobooks

igloobooks

Published in 2015
by Igloo Books Ltd
Cottage Farm
Sywell
NN6 0BJ
www.igloobooks.com

Food photography and recipe development: PhotoCuisine UK
Front and back cover images © PhotoCuisine UK

HUN001 0715
4 6 8 10 9 7 5
ISBN: 978-1-78343-529-6

Printed and manufactured in China

Contents

Classics

Lemon and Poppy Seed Cupcakes

MAKES 12

PREPARATION TIME 45 MINUTES

COOKING TIME 15–20 MINUTES

INGREDIENTS

110 g / 4 oz / ⅔ cup self-raising flour, sifted

110 g / 4 oz / ½ cup caster (superfine) sugar

110 g / 4 oz / ½ cup butter, softened

½ lemon, juiced and zest finely grated

2 large eggs

TO DECORATE

100 g / 3 ½ oz / ½ cup butter, softened

200 g / 7 oz / 2 cups icing (confectioners') sugar

a few drops of pale yellow food dye

2 tsp lemon juice

2 tbsp poppy seeds

METHOD

- Preheat the oven to 190°C (170°C fan) / 375F / gas 5 and line a 12-hole cupcake tin with paper cases.

- Whisk the cake ingredients together until smooth and light. Divide the mixture between the paper cases and bake for 15–20 minutes or until a toothpick inserted into the centre comes out clean. Leave to cool completely.

- Whisk the butter until smooth, then gradually incorporate the icing sugar and lemon juice and food dye and whip for 2 minutes.

- Spoon the icing into a piping bag fitted with a large star nozzle and pipe a swirl on top of each cake. Sprinkle with poppy seeds.

TOP TIP
Stir 1 tbsp of poppy seeds through the cake mixture for extra crunch.

Macchiato Cupcakes

MAKES 12

PREPARATION TIME 45 MINUTES

COOKING TIME 15–18 MINUTES

INGREDIENTS

110 g / 4 oz / ⅔ cup self-raising flour, sifted

110 g / 4 oz / ½ cup margarine

110 g / 4 oz / ½ cup caster (superfine) sugar

55 g / 2 oz / ⅓ cup cocoa powder

55 ml / 2 fl. oz / ¼ cup whole milk

2 large eggs

a pinch of salt

TO DECORATE

100 g / 3 ½ oz / ½ cup butter, softened

200 g / 7 oz / 2 cups icing (confectioners') sugar

1 tbsp cocoa powder

1 tsp strong instant espresso powder

12 chocolate balls

METHOD

- Preheat the oven to 180°C (160°C fan) / 350F / gas 4 and line a 12-hole cupcake tin with 12 cupcake cases.

- Beat together all the ingredients for the batter apart from the milk in a mixing bowl for 2 minutes.

- Add the milk and beat again for a further minute.

- Divide evenly between the paper cases.

- Bake for 15–18 minutes until risen or until a toothpick inserted into the centre comes out clean.

- Remove to a wire rack to cool.

- Beat the softened butter with the icing sugar until smooth.

- Add the cocoa powder and espresso powder and beat again.

- Spoon about one third of the buttercream into a piping bag fitted with a star-shaped nozzle.

- Spread the tops of the cupcakes evenly with the remaining buttercream.

- Pipe a swirl of buttercream on top of the flat icing before garnishing the top with a chocolate ball.

TOP TIP
Top the cakes with chocolate-coated coffee beans for an extra hit of coffee.

Raspberry Yoghurt Cupcakes

MAKES 12

PREPARATION TIME 45 MINUTES

COOKING TIME 15–18 MINUTES

INGREDIENTS

110 g / 4 oz / ⅔ cup self-raising flour, sifted

110 g / 4 oz / ½ cup margarine

110 g / 4 oz / ½ cup caster (superfine) sugar

1 tsp vanilla extract

2 large eggs

a pinch of salt

TO DECORATE

100 g / 3 ½ oz / ½ cup butter, softened

200 g / 7 oz / 2 cups icing (confectioners')
    sugar

4 tbsp thick raspberry yoghurt

1 tsp vanilla extract

12 raspberries

½ tsp pink edible glitter

METHOD

- Preheat the oven to 180°C (160°C fan) / 350F / gas 4 and line a 12-hole cupcake tin with 12 cupcake cases.

- Beat together all the ingredients for the batter in a mixing bowl for 2 minutes until smooth and creamy.

- Divide evenly between the paper cases before rapping the tin on a work surface to help settle the batter.

- Bake for 15–18 minutes until risen.

- Remove to a wire rack to cool.

- Beat the softened butter for 3–4 minutes until creamy.

- Add the icing sugar, vanilla yoghurt and vanilla extract before beating again until smooth.

- Spoon into a piping bag fitted with a petal tip before piping petals on top to form roses.

- Garnish with a light dusting of the glitter and a raspberry in the middle.

TOP TIP
Try plain yoghurt drizzled with honey for a fresh topping.

Candied Orange Cream Cupcakes

MAKES 12

PREPARATION TIME 40 MINUTES

COOKING TIME 15–20 MINUTES

INGREDIENTS

110 g / 4 oz / ⅔ cup self-raising flour, sifted

110 g / 4 oz / ½ cup caster (superfine) sugar

110 g / 4 oz / ½ cup butter, softened

1 tsp finely grated orange zest

2 large eggs

50 g / 1 ¾ oz / ⅓ cup candied orange peel, chopped

TO DECORATE

400 ml / 14 fl. oz / 1 ⅔ cups double (heavy) cream

2 tbsp candied orange peel, chopped

12 candied orange slices

METHOD

- Preheat the oven to 190°C (170°C fan) / 375F / gas 5 and line a 12-hole cupcake tin with paper cases.

- Measure the cake ingredients into a bowl then whisk together for 3 minutes or until smooth and light. Divide the mixture between the paper cases, then transfer the tin to the oven and bake for 15–20 minutes.

- Test the cakes with a toothpick inserted into the centre; if it comes out clean, the cakes are done. Transfer the cakes to a wire rack and leave to cool completely.

- Whip the cream until it holds its shape, then pipe a swirl on top of each cake. Sprinkle the cakes with the chopped peel, then top each one with a whole candied orange slice.

TOP TIP

These cakes are also delicious decorated with candied lemon slices.

Vanilla Cream Raspberry Cupcakes

MAKES 12

PREPARATION TIME 30 MINUTES

COOKING TIME 20 MINUTES

INGREDIENTS

125 g / 4 ½ oz / ½ cup unsalted butter, softened

125 g / 4 ½ oz / ½ cup caster (superfine) sugar

2 medium eggs

½ tsp vanilla extract

125 g / 4 ½ oz / 1 cup self-raising flour

2 tbsp cocoa powder

45 ml / 1 ½ fl. oz / ¼ cup milk

TO DECORATE

125 g / 4 ½ oz / ½ cup unsalted butter, softened

300 g / 10 ½ oz / 2 ½ cups icing (confectioners') sugar

½ tsp vanilla extract

½ tbsp milk

12 raspberries

METHOD

- Preheat the oven to 180°C (160°C fan) / 350F / gas 4 and line a cupcake tin with paper cases.

- Cream the butter and sugar until pale and fluffy with an electric whisk.

- Gradually mix in the egg and vanilla extract.

- Gently mix in the flour and cocoa, adding the milk.

- Spoon the cupcake mix into each paper case.

- Bake for 18–20 minutes. Test with a wooden toothpick inserted into the centre, if it comes out clean, the cakes are done.

- Place on a wire rack to cool.

- To make the buttercream, beat the butter with a whisk until soft then gradually beat in the icing sugar, vanilla and milk.

- Spoon the buttercream into a piping bag fitted with a large plain nozzle and pipe onto the cupcakes. Decorate each one with a raspberry.

TOP TIP

Try folding a handful of raspberries through the cake mixture for a burst of fruit.

White-choc Coffee Cupcakes

MAKES 12

PREPARATION TIME 45 MINUTES

COOKING TIME 15–18 MINUTES

INGREDIENTS

110 g / 4 oz / ⅔ cup self-raising flour, sifted

110 g / 4 oz / ½ cup margarine

110 g / 4 oz / ½ cup caster (superfine) sugar

1 tsp vanilla extract

2 large eggs, a pinch of salt

VANILLA BUTTERCREAM

175 g / 6 oz / ¾ cup unsalted butter

125 g / 4 ½ oz / 1 cup icing (confectioners') sugar

1 tsp vanilla extract

TO DECORATE

100 g / 3 ½ oz / ½ cup butter, softened

200 g / 7 oz / 2 cups icing (confectioners') sugar

1 tsp vanilla extract

1 tsp instant espresso powder

12 white chocolate buttons

METHOD

- Preheat the oven to 180°C (160°C fan) / 350F / gas 4 and line a 12-hole cupcake tin with 12 cupcake cases.

- Beat together all the ingredients for the batter in a mixing bowl for 2 minutes until smooth and creamy.

- Divide evenly between the paper cases.

- Bake for 15–18 minutes until risen. Test with a wooden toothpick inserted into the centre; if it comes out clean the cakes are done.

- Beat the softened butter with the icing sugar and vanilla extract until smooth and set to one side.

- For the coffee decoration, beat together the butter for the buttercream with the icing sugar for the coffee buttercream; mix together the espresso powder with 1 tbsp of boiling water before beating into the butter, making sure you leave it rippled.

- Spoon into a piping bag fitted with a round nozzle.

- Spread the tops of the cupcakes with the vanilla buttercream before piping a round of icing on top.

- Garnish with a white chocolate button.

TOP TIP

Fold 75 g of white chocolate chips through the cake mixture for a touch of luxury.

Violet Sprinkle Cupcakes

MAKES 12

PREPARATION TIME 30 MINUTES

COOKING TIME 15–18 MINUTES

INGREDIENTS

110 g / 4 oz / ⅔ cup self-raising flour, sifted

110 g / 4 oz / ½ cup margarine, softened

110 g / 4 oz / ½ cup caster (superfine) sugar

1 tsp vanilla extract

2 large eggs

a pinch of salt

TO DECORATE

100 g / 3 ½ oz / ½ cup butter, softened

200 g / 7 oz / 2 cups icing (confectioners') sugar

1 tsp vanilla extract

a few drops of purple food dye

1 tbsp purple sugar sprinkles

METHOD

- Preheat the oven to 180°C (160°C fan) / 350F / gas 4 and line a 12-hole cupcake tin with 12 cupcake cases.

- Beat together all the ingredients for the batter in a mixing bowl for 2 minutes until smooth and creamy.

- Divide evenly between the paper cases before rapping the tin on a work surface to help settle the batter.

- Bake for 15–18 minutes until risen; test with a wooden toothpick inserted into the centre; if it comes out clean, the cakes are done.

- Remove to a wire rack to cool as you prepare the buttercream.

- Beat the softened butter in a mixing bowl for 3–4 minutes until pale.

- Add the icing sugar and vanilla extract, beating well before spooning a quarter of it into a piping bag fitted with a plain nozzle.

- Add drops of the food dye to the remaining buttercream, beating well until violet.

- Spread evenly on top of the cupcakes using a small palette knife.

- Pipe a blob of icing from the piping bag on top and garnish with a sprinkle of sugar sprinkles.

TOP TIP
Replace the food dye and vanilla extract with 2 tbsp of violet syrup.

Girly Buttercream Cupcakes

MAKES 12

PREPARATION TIME 40 MINUTES

COOKING TIME 10–15 MINUTES

INGREDIENTS

110 g / 4 oz / 1 cup self-raising flour, sifted

110 g / 4 oz / ½ cup caster (superfine) sugar

110 g / 4 oz / ½ cup butter, softened

2 large eggs

1 tsp vanilla extract

TO DECORATE:

110 g / 4 oz / ½ cup butter, softened

225 g / 8 oz / 2 cups icing (confectioners')
    sugar, plus extra for dusting

2 tbsp milk

1 tsp vanilla extract

12 heart-shaped sweets

clear sugar crystal sprinkles to decorate

METHOD

- Preheat the oven to 190°C (170°C fan) / 375F / gas 5 and line a 12-hole cupcake tin with paper cases.

- Combine the flour, sugar, butter, eggs and vanilla extract in a bowl and whisk together for 2 minutes or until smooth.

- Divide the mixture between the cake cases then transfer the tin to the oven and bake for 10–15 minutes. Test with a wooden toothpick inserted into the centre; if it comes out clean, the cakes are done. Transfer the cakes to a wire rack and leave to cool completely.

- To make the buttercream, beat the butter until smooth then beat in the icing sugar. Use a whisk to incorporate the milk and vanilla extract, then whisk for 2 minutes or until well whipped.

- Spoon the icing into a piping bag fitted with a large plain nozzle and pipe it onto the cakes. Top each one with a sweet and sprinkle with sugar crystals.

TOP TIP
Replace the buttercream with mini marshmallows for a fluffy finish.

Lavender Pillow Cupcakes

MAKES 12

PREPARATION TIME 30 MINUTES

COOKING TIME 15–18 MINUTES

INGREDIENTS

110 g / 4 oz / ⅔ cup self-raising flour, sifted

110 g / 4 oz / ½ cup margarine, softened

110 g / 4 oz / ½ cup caster (superfine) sugar

1 tsp lemon extract

2 large eggs

a pinch of salt

TO DECORATE

100 g / 3 ½ oz / ½ cup butter, softened

200 g / 7 oz / 2 cups icing (confectioners')
   sugar

½ tsp vanilla extract

½ tsp edible lavender extract

a few drops of purple food dye

1 tbsp lavender sugar

METHOD

- Preheat the oven to 190°C (170°C fan) / 375F / gas 5 and line a 12-hole cupcake tin with paper cases.

- Combine the cake ingredients and whisk together for 2 minutes.

- Divide the mixture between the cases and bake for 15–18 minutes.

- Test with a wooden toothpick inserted into the centre; if it comes out clean, the cakes are done.

- Transfer the cakes to a wire rack and leave to cool.

- Beat the butter with the icing sugar, vanilla extract and lavender extract until smooth then set aside two thirds of the icing.

- Dye the remaining icing pale purple and spread it over the cakes.

- Pipe the reserved white icing onto the cakes and dip the tops in lavender sugar.

TOP TIP
Sprigs of fresh lavender flowers make a pretty decoration for these cakes.

Crimson Raspberry Cupcakes

MAKES 12

PREPARATION TIME 45 MINUTES

COOKING TIME 15–18 MINUTES

INGREDIENTS

FOR THE BATTER

110 g / 4 oz / ⅔ cup self-raising flour, sifted

110 g / 4 oz / ½ cup margarine, softened

110 g / 4 oz / ½ cup caster (superfine) sugar

1 tsp vanilla extract

2 medium eggs

a pinch of salt

a few drops of red food dye

3 tbsp framboise liqueur

TO DECORATE

100 g / 3 ½ oz / ½ cup butter, softened

200 g / 7 oz / 2 cups icing (confectioners') sugar

1 tsp vanilla extract

12 raspberries

METHOD

- Preheat the oven to 180°C (160°C fan) / 350F / gas 4 and line a 12-hole cupcake tin with 12 cupcake cases.

- Beat together all the ingredients for the batter apart from the food dye in a mixing bowl for 2 minutes.

- Add drops of food dye, beating well, until you have a pink batter.

- Divide evenly between the paper cases and bake for 15–18 minutes until risen. When a toothpick inserted into the centre; if it comes out clean the cakes are done.

- Remove to a wire rack to cool.

- Beat the softened butter for 3–4 minutes until creamy and pale.

- Add the icing sugar and vanilla extract and beat until smooth.

- Spoon into a piping bag fitted with a plain nozzle before piping pillows of buttercream on top.

- Garnish with a raspberry on top of the cakes.

TOP TIP

Replace the framboise with raspberry syrup for a non-alcoholic version.

Kiwi and Lime Cupcakes

MAKES 12

PREPARATION TIME 35 MINUTES

COOKING TIME 15–18 MINUTES

INGREDIENTS

110 g / 4 oz / ⅔ cup self-raising flour, sifted

110 g / 4 oz / ½ cup margarine, softened

110 g / 4 oz / ½ cup caster (superfine) sugar

1 tsp vanilla extract

2 large eggs

a pinch of salt

TO DECORATE

100 g / 3 ½ oz / ½ cup butter, softened

200 g / 7 oz / 2 cups icing (confectioners')
    sugar

2 tbsp lime cordial

1 kiwi fruit, cut into 12 semi-circles

METHOD

- Preheat the oven to 180°C (160°C fan) / 350F / gas 4 and line a 12-hole cupcake tin with 12 cupcake cases.

- Beat together all the ingredients for the batter in a mixing bowl for 2 minutes until smooth and creamy.

- Divide evenly between the paper cases before rapping the tin on a work surface to help settle the batter.

- Bake for 15–18 minutes until risen; test with a wooden toothpick inserted into the centre; if it comes out clean, the cakes are done.

- Remove to a wire rack to cool as you prepare the buttercream.

- Beat the softened butter for 2 minutes until creamy and pale.

- Add the icing sugar and lime cordial and beat well until smooth.

- Spoon into a piping bag fitted with a star-shaped nozzle before levelling the cupcakes.

- Pipe a flat swirl on top of the cupcakes before garnishing with a semi-circle of kiwi fruit.

TOP TIP
Try 1 tsp lime zest instead of the vanilla extract, for a citrus twist.

Chocolate Lime Cupcakes

MAKES 12

PREPARATION TIME 45 MINUTES

COOKING TIME 15–18 MINUTES

INGREDIENTS

FOR THE BATTER

110 g / 4 oz / ⅔ cup self-raising flour, sifted

110 g / 4 oz / ½ cup margarine, softened

110 g / 4 oz / ½ cup caster (superfine) sugar

2 tbsp cocoa powder

2 tbsp whole milk

2 large eggs

a pinch of salt

TO DECORATE

100 g / 3 ½ oz / ½ cup butter, softened

200 g / 7 oz / 2 cups icing (confectioners')
    sugar

2 tbsp lime cordial

36 lime jelly beans

½ tsp edible glitter

METHOD

- Preheat the oven to 180°C (160°C fan) / 350F / gas 4 and line a 12-hole cupcake tin with 12 cupcake cases.

- Beat together all the ingredients for the batter in a mixing bowl for 2 minutes until smooth and creamy.

- Divide evenly between the paper cases before rapping the tin on a work surface to help settle the batter.

- Bake for 15–18 minutes until risen; test with a wooden toothpick inserted into the centre; if it comes out clean, the cakes are done.

- Remove to a wire rack to cool as you prepare the buttercream.

- Beat the softened butter for 2 minutes until creamy and pale.

- Add the icing sugar and lime cordial and beat well until smooth before spooning into a piping bag fitted with a petal tip.

- Garnish the tops of the cupcakes with a little glitter before piping a ruffled mound of lime buttercream on top.

- Garnish with 3 jelly beans on top of each cake.

TOP TIP
Add the finely grated zest of a lime to the cake mixture for extra lime flavour.

Peppermint Sugar Cupcakes

MAKES 12

PREPARATION TIME 30 MINUTES

COOKING TIME 15–18 MINUTES

INGREDIENTS

110 g / 4 oz / ⅔ cup self-raising flour, sifted

110 g / 4 oz / ½ cup margarine, softened

110 g / 4 oz / ½ cup caster (superfine) sugar

1 tsp vanilla extract

2 large eggs

a pinch of salt

TO DECORATE

200 g / 7 oz / 1 cup butter, softened

400 g / 14 oz / 4 cups icing (confectioners') sugar

a few drops of peppermint essence

a few drops of green food dye

1 tbsp green sugar sprinkles

METHOD

- Preheat the oven to 180°C (160°C fan) / 350F / gas 4 and line a 12-hole cupcake tin with 12 cupcake cases.

- Beat together all the ingredients for the batter.

- Divide evenly between the paper cases.

- Bake for 15–18 minutes until risen. Test with a wooden toothpick inserted into the centre; if it comes out clean the cakes are done. Transfer the cakes to a wire rack and leave to cool.

- Beat the butter with the icing sugar, peppermint essence and food dye until smooth.

- Set aside half of the buttercream and spread the rest over the cakes. Sprinkle with green sugar.

- Pipe the reserved buttercream around the edge of the cakes.

TOP TIP

Stir 1 tbsp of finely chopped peppermint leaves through the cake mixture.

Blueberry Cinnamon Cupcakes

MAKES 12
PREPARATION TIME 30 MINUTES
COOKING TIME 15–18 MINUTES

INGREDIENTS

110 g / 4 oz / ⅔ cup self-raising flour, sifted
110 g / 4 oz / ½ cup margarine, softened
110 g / 4 oz / ½ cup caster (superfine) sugar
1 tsp vanilla extract
1 tsp ground cinnamon
2 large eggs
1 pinch of salt

TO DECORATE

225 g / 8 oz / 1 cup cream cheese
180 g / 6 oz / 1 ½ cups icing (confectioners')
    sugar
1 tbsp lemon juice
a few drops of purple food dye
300 g / 7 oz / 2 cups blueberries

METHOD

- Preheat the oven to 180°C (160°C fan) / 350F / gas 4 and line a 12-hole cupcake tin with 12 cupcake cases.

- Beat together all the ingredients for the batter in a mixing bowl for 2 minutes until smooth and creamy.

- Divide evenly between the paper cases before rapping the tin on a work surface to help settle the batter.

- Bake for 15–18 minutes until risen; test with a wooden toothpick inserted into the centre; if it comes out clean, the cakes are done.

- Remove to a wire rack to cool as you prepare the icing.

- Beat the cream cheese with the icing sugar, lemon juice and drops of food dye until you have an even purple icing.

- Spoon into a piping bag fitted with a large plain nozzle before piping spiral swirls on the cupcakes.

- Garnish the perimeter with blueberries before serving.

TOP TIP
Finish the cakes with a sprinkle of ground cinnamon for a great aroma.

35

Lemon Meringue Cupcakes

MAKES 12

PREPARATION TIME 50 MINUTES

COOKING TIME 15–20 MINUTES

INGREDIENTS

110 g / 4 oz / ⅔ cup self-raising flour, sifted

110 g / 4 oz / ½ cup caster (superfine) sugar

110 g / 4 oz / ½ cup butter, softened

2 large eggs

1 lemon, juiced and zest finely grated

TO DECORATE

100 g / 3 ½ oz / ½ cup lemon curd

200 g / 7 oz / 2 cups marshmallow fluff

1 lemon, cut into 12 wedges

METHOD

- Preheat the oven to 190°C (170°C fan) / 375F / gas 5 and line a 12-hole cupcake tin with paper cases.

- Combine the flour, sugar, butter, eggs and lemon juice and zest in a bowl and whisk for 2 minutes or until smooth. Divide the mixture between the cases, then transfer the tin to the oven and bake for 15–20 minutes or until a toothpick inserted into the centre comes out clean.

- Transfer the cakes to a wire rack and leave to cool.

- Use an apple corer to remove the centre of each cupcake.

- Fill the cavity in each cupcake with a heaped teaspoon of lemon curd.

- Spoon the marshmallow fluff into a piping bag and cover the surface of the cakes with small teardrops.

- Use a fork to rough up the top, making sure there are no gaps.

- Use a blowtorch to toast the marshmallow topping then top each one with a wedge of lemon.

TOP TIP

Whisk 100 g of caster sugar into 4 stiffly beaten egg whites for the topping.

Lime Green Sugar Cupcakes

MAKES 12

PREPARATION TIME 45 MINUTES

COOKING TIME 15–20 MINUTES

INGREDIENTS

110 g / 4 oz / ⅔ cup self-raising flour, sifted

110 g / 4 oz / ½ cup caster (superfine) sugar

110 g / 4 oz / ½ cup butter, softened

2 large eggs

1 lime, juiced and zest finely grated

TO DECORATE

100 g / 3 ½ oz / ½ cup butter, softened

200 g / 7 oz / 2 cups icing (confectioners') sugar

1 lime, juiced and zest finely grated

green food dye

green sugar sprinkles

METHOD

- Preheat the oven to 190°C (170°C fan) / 375F / gas 5 and line a 12-hole cupcake tin with paper cases.

- Combine the flour, sugar, butter, eggs and lime juice and zest in a bowl and whisk together for 2 minutes or until smooth. Divide the mixture between the cases, then transfer the tin to the oven and bake for 15–20 minutes.

- Test with a wooden toothpick inserted into the centre; if it comes out clean, the cakes are done. Transfer the cakes to a wire rack and leave to cool completely.

- Beat the butter until smooth, then gradually whisk in the icing sugar, lime juice and zest and a little green food dye.

- Spoon the mixture into a piping bag, fitted with a large star nozzle and pipe a swirl of buttercream on top of each cake.

- Sprinkle the cupcakes generously with green sugar sprinkles.

TOP TIP

For vibrant cakes, add a few drops of green food dye to the cake mixture.

39

Nectarine and Lemon Cupcakes

MAKES 12

PREPARATION TIME 45 MINUTES

COOKING TIME 15–20 MINUTES

INGREDIENTS

110 g / 4 oz / ⅔ cup self-raising flour, sifted

110 g / 4 oz / ½ cup caster (superfine) sugar

110 g / 4 oz / ½ cup butter, softened

2 large eggs

2 nectarines, stoned and finely chopped

TO DECORATE

100 g / 3 ½ oz / ½ cup butter, softened

200 g / 7 oz / 2 cups icing (confectioners') sugar

½ lemon, juiced and zest finely grated

orange sugar pearls

METHOD

- Preheat the oven to 190°C (170°C fan) / 375F / gas 5 and line a 12-hole cupcake tin with paper cases.

- Combine the flour, sugar, butter and eggs in a bowl and whisk together for 2 minutes or until smooth. Fold in the nectarines then divide the mixture between the cases and bake for 15–20 minutes.

- Test with a wooden toothpick inserted into the centre; if it comes out clean, the cakes are done. Transfer the cakes to a wire rack and leave to cool completely.

- Beat the butter until smooth, then gradually whisk in the icing sugar, lemon juice and zest.

- Spoon the mixture into a piping bag, fitted with a large star nozzle and pipe a swirl of buttercream on top of each cake.

- Sprinkle the cupcakes generously with orange sugar pearls.

TOP TIP
Decorate the cakes with nectarine slices for a fresh and fruity finish.

Vintage Rose Cupcakes

MAKES 12

PREPARATION TIME 1 HOUR

COOKING TIME 15–20 MINUTES

INGREDIENTS

110 g / 4 oz / ⅔ cup self-raising flour, sifted

110 g / 4 oz / ½ cup caster (superfine) sugar

110 g / 4 oz / ½ cup butter, softened

2 large eggs

2 tbsp unsweetened cocoa powder

TO DECORATE

200 g / 7 oz / ½ cup ready-to-roll fondant
    icing

blue pearlescent dusting powder

METHOD

- Preheat the oven to 190°C (170°C fan) / 375F / gas 5. Line a cupcake tin with 12 paper cases.

- Combine the flour, sugar, butter, eggs and cocoa in a bowl and whisk for 2 minutes. Divide between the cases, then transfer to the oven and bake for 15–20 minutes or until a toothpick inserted into the centre comes out clean.

- Transfer the cakes to a wire rack and leave to cool completely.

- Dust the work surface lightly with icing sugar and roll out the icing.

- Dust a rose-shaped embossing tool with icing sugar.

- Press the embossing tool into the surface of the icing, being careful not to cut all the way through.

- Repeat until the surface of the icing is filled with roses.

- Use a cookie cutter the same diameter as the top of the cakes to cut out 12 circles.

- Using a dry paint brush, work a little blue pearlescent dusting powder into the embossed lines.

- Attach an icing circle to the top of each cake, using a dab of water to secure.

TOP TIP

Look out for lace embossing tools and make vintage lace cupcakes.

Flower Sprinkle Cupcakes

MAKES 12
PREPARATION TIME 45 MINUTES
COOKING TIME 15–18 MINUTES

INGREDIENTS

110 g / 4 oz / ⅔ cup self-raising flour, sifted

110 g / 4 oz / ½ cup caster (superfine) sugar

110 g / 4 oz / ½ cup butter, softened

a few drops of lavender syrup

1 tbsp rose water

2 large eggs

TO DECORATE

200 g / 7 oz / 1 cup butter, softened

400 g / 14 oz / 4 cups icing (confectioners')
    sugar

a few drops of lavender syrup

2 tsp rose water

purple sugar strands

12 sugar flowers

METHOD

- Preheat the oven to 190°C (170°C fan) / 375F / gas 5 and line a 12-hole cupcake tin with paper cases.

- Measure the cake ingredients into a bowl then whisk together for 3 minutes or until smooth and light. Divide the mixture between the paper cases, then transfer the tin to the oven and bake for 15–20 minutes.

- Test the cakes with a toothpick inserted into the centre; if it comes out clean, the cakes are done. Transfer the cakes to a wire rack and leave to cool completely.

- Whisk the butter until smooth, then gradually incorporate the icing sugar, lavender syrup and rose water. Whisk for 2 minutes or until light and fluffy.

- Spoon the buttercream into a piping bag fitted with a large star nozzle and pipe a big swirl onto each cake. Decorate each one with purple sugar strands and a flower.

TOP TIP
Try adding a few drops of orange flower water to the cake mixture and icing.

Lavender Cupcakes

MAKES 12

PREPARATION TIME 1 HOUR

COOKING TIME 15–20 MINUTES

INGREDIENTS

110 g / 4 oz / ⅔ cup self-raising flour, sifted
110 g / 4 oz / ½ cup caster (superfine) sugar
110 g / 4 oz / ½ cup butter, softened
few drops of lavender syrup
2 large eggs

TO DECORATE

1 egg white
200 g / 7 oz / 2 cups icing (confectioners')
    sugar, sieved
few drops of lavender syrup
36 lavender sprigs
12 purple ribbons

METHOD

- Preheat the oven to 190°C (170°C fan) / 375F / gas 5 and line a 12-hole cupcake tin with paper cases.

- Whisk the cake ingredients together for 3 minutes or until smooth. Divide the mixture between the paper cases and bake for 15–20 minutes.

- Test the cakes with a toothpick inserted into the centre; if it comes out clean, the cakes are done. Leave to cool completely.

- Whisk the egg white until foamy, then gradually incorporate the icing sugar and lavender syrup and whip for 3 minutes. Add cold water a few drops at a time until it reaches the texture of thick double cream, then spread it over the cakes.

- Tie the lavender sprigs together in bundles of 3 with the ribbons, then add a posy to the top of each cake.

TOP TIP

Add the finely grated zest of a lemon to the cake mixture for a citrus twist.

Banoffee Cupcakes

MAKES 12

PREPARATION TIME 40 MINUTES

COOKING TIME 15–20 MINUTES

INGREDIENTS

110 g / 4 oz / ⅔ cup self-raising flour, sifted
110 g / 4 oz / ½ cup caster (superfine) sugar
110 g / 4 oz / ½ cup butter, softened
2 large eggs
1 large banana, finely chopped

TO DECORATE

400 ml / 14 fl. oz / 1 ⅔ cups double (heavy)
    cream
3 tbsp dulce de leche
75 g / 2 ½ oz / ½ cup fudge pieces
1 large banana, sliced
yellow sugar strands

METHOD

- Preheat the oven to 190°C (170°C fan) / 375F / gas 5 and line a 12-hole cupcake tin with paper cases.

- Measure the cake ingredients into a bowl then whisk together for 3 minutes or until smooth and light. Divide the mixture between the paper cases and bake for 15–20 minutes or until a skewer inserted into the centre comes out clean. Leave to cool completely.

- Whip the cream until it holds its shape, then pipe a swirl on top of each cake.

- Drizzle the cakes with dulce de leche and scatter over the fudge pieces. Top each cake with a banana slice and sprinkle with yellow sugar strands.

TOP TIP
Try topping the cakes with banana curd before piping on the cream.

Orange and Poppy Seed Cupcakes

MAKES 12

PREPARATION TIME 45 MINUTES

COOKING TIME 15–20 MINUTES

INGREDIENTS

110 g / 4 oz / ⅔ cup self-raising flour, sifted
110 g / 4 oz / ½ cup caster (superfine) sugar
110 g / 4 oz / ½ cup butter, softened
½ orange, juiced and zest finely grated
2 large eggs

TO DECORATE

100 g / 3 ½ oz / ½ cup butter, softened
200 g / 7 oz / 2 cups icing (confectioners')
    sugar
1 orange, juiced and zest finely pared
2 tbsp poppy seeds

METHOD

- Preheat the oven to 190°C (170°C fan) / 375F / gas 5 and line a 12-hole cupcake tin with paper cases.

- Whisk the cake ingredients together until smooth and light. Divide the mixture between the paper cases and bake for 15–20 minutes or until a toothpick inserted into the centre comes out clean. Leave to cool completely.

- Whisk the butter until smooth, then gradually incorporate the icing sugar and 2 tsp of the orange juice.

- Fit a piping bag with a large plain nozzle and pipe a swirl on top of each cake. Sprinkle with poppy seeds and top with the orange zest.

TOP TIP
Fold 3 tbsp of marmalade through the buttercream for a bittersweet tangy flavour.

51

Indulgent

White-choc Raspberry Cupcakes

MAKES 12

PREPARATION TIME 1 HOUR

COOKING TIME 15–20 MINUTES

INGREDIENTS

110 g / 4 oz / ⅔ cup self-raising flour, sifted

110 g / 4 oz / ½ cup caster (superfine) sugar

110 g / 4 oz / ½ cup butter, softened

2 large eggs

1 tsp vanilla extract

TO DECORATE

100 g / 3 ½ oz / ½ cup butter, softened

200 g / 7 oz / 2 cups icing (confectioners')
   sugar

1 tsp vanilla extract

4 tbsp raspberry jam (jelly)

96 white chocolate buttons

36 raspberries

METHOD

- Preheat the oven to 190°C (170°C fan) /
  375F / gas 5 and line a 12-hole cupcake tin
  with paper cases.

- Combine the flour, sugar, butter, eggs and
  vanilla extract in a bowl and whisk for
  2 minutes or until smooth. Divide
  the mixture between the cases, then
  transfer the tin to the oven and bake for
  15–20 minutes or until a toothpick
  inserted into the centre comes out clean.

- Transfer the cakes to a wire rack and leave
  to cool.

- Beat the butter until smooth, then
  gradually whisk in the icing sugar and
  vanilla extract.

- Swirl through half of the raspberry jam.

- Spread the buttercream onto the cakes.

- Make an indent in the top of the icing with
  a teaspoon.

- Press 8 white chocolate buttons into the
  icing round the edge of each cake.

- Fill the indentation in the icing with the
  rest of the raspberry jam and top each one
  with 3 raspberries.

TOP TIP

Try folding a handful of
white chocolate chips
through the
cake mixture.

Chocolate Kiwi Mud Cupcakes

MAKES 12

PREPARATION TIME 30 MINUTES

COOKING TIME 15–18 MINUTES

INGREDIENTS

110 g / 4 oz / ⅔ cup self-raising flour, sifted

110 g / 4 oz / ½ cup margarine, softened

110 g / 4 oz / ½ cup caster (superfine) sugar

55 g / 2 oz / ⅓ cup cocoa powder

55 ml / 2 fl. oz / ¼ cup whole milk

2 large eggs, a pinch of salt

TO DECORATE

200 g / 7 oz / 1 cup butter, softened

400 g / 14 oz / 4 cups icing (confectioners')
    sugar

2 tbsp cocoa powder, plus extra for dusting

1 tbsp milk

3 kiwi fruit, peeled and chopped

12 chocolate shapes

METHOD

- Preheat the oven to 190°C (170°C fan) / 375F / gas 5 and line a 12-hole cupcake tin with paper cases.

- Combine the cake ingredients and whisk together until smooth.

- Divide the mixture between the cases and bake for 15–20 minutes or until a toothpick inserted into the centre comes out clean.

- Transfer the cakes to a wire rack and leave to cool.

- Beat the butter with the icing sugar, cocoa and milk until smooth then pipe it onto the cakes.

- Sprinkle with cocoa powder, then arrange the chopped kiwi round the outside and garnish with a chocolate shape.

TOP TIP

Make your own shapes by piping melted chocolate onto greaseproof paper.

Vanilla Daisy Cupcakes

MAKES 12

PREPARATION TIME 45 MINUTES

COOKING TIME 15–20 MINUTES

INGREDIENTS

110 g / 4 oz / ⅔ cup self-raising flour, sifted

110 g / 4 oz / ½ cup caster (superfine) sugar

110 g / 4 oz / ½ cup butter, softened

1 tsp vanilla extract

2 large eggs

TO DECORATE

100 g / 3 ½ oz / ½ cup butter, softened

200 g / 7 oz / 2 cups icing (confectioners')
    sugar

1 tsp vanilla extract

12 sugar daisies

METHOD

- Preheat the oven to 190°C (170°C fan) / 375F / gas 5 and line a 12-hole cupcake tin with paper cases.

- Whisk the cake ingredients together until smooth and light. Divide the mixture between the paper cases and bake for 15–20 minutes or until a toothpick inserted into the centre comes out clean. Leave to cool completely.

- Whisk the butter until smooth, then gradually incorporate the icing sugar and vanilla extract and whip for 2 minutes.

- Spoon the buttercream into a piping bag fitted with a large star nozzle and pipe a swirl onto each cake. Top with the sugar daisies.

TOP TIP

Make your own daisies with white and yellow fondant icing and a silicone mould.

Chocolate, Raspberry and Kiwi Cupcakes

MAKES 12

PREPARATION TIME 30 MINUTES

COOKING TIME 15–18 MINUTES

INGREDIENTS

110 g / 4 oz / ⅔ cup self-raising flour, sifted
110 g / 4 oz / ½ cup margarine
110 g / 4 oz / ½ cup caster (superfine) sugar
1 tsp vanilla extract
2 large eggs

TO DECORATE

250 ml / 9 fl. oz / 1 cup double (heavy) cream
65 g / 2 ½ oz / ½ cup icing (confectioners')
    sugar
1 tsp vanilla extract
12 raspberries
12 chocolate cigarillos
12 sprigs of mint leaves
1 kiwi fruit, cut into 12 semi-circles

METHOD

- Preheat the oven to 180°C (160°C fan) / 350F / gas 4 and line a 12-hole cupcake tin with 12 cupcake cases.

- Beat together all the ingredients for the batter in a mixing bowl for 2 minutes until smooth and creamy.

- Divide evenly between the paper cases before rapping the tin on a work surface to help settle the batter.

- Bake for 15–18 minutes until risen; test with a wooden toothpick inserted into the centre; if it comes out clean, the cakes are done.

- Remove to a wire rack to cool as you prepare the cream.

- Whip the cream with the icing sugar and vanilla extract until almost clotted.

- Spoon on top of the cupcakes and garnish with the fruit, mint and cigarillos.

TOP TIP
Add 2 tbsp of unsweetened cocoa powder to the cake mixture.

Sugared Blueberry Cupcakes

MAKES 12

PREPARATION TIME 30 MINUTES

COOKING TIME 15–18 MINUTES

INGREDIENTS

110 g / 4 oz / ⅔ cup self-raising flour, sifted

110 g / 4 oz / ½ cup margarine, softened

110 g / 4 oz / ½ cup caster (superfine) sugar

1 tsp vanilla extract

2 large eggs

a pinch of salt

TO DECORATE

100 g / 3 ½ oz / ½ cup unsalted butter, softened

200 g / 7 oz / 2 cup icing (confectioners') sugar

a few drops of purple food dye

150 g / 5 oz / 1 ½ cups blueberries

1 tbsp caster (superfine) sugar

METHOD

- Preheat the oven to 180°C (160°C fan) / 350F / gas 4 and line a 12-hole cupcake tin with 12 cupcake cases.

- Beat together all the ingredients for the batter in a mixing bowl for 2 minutes until smooth and creamy.

- Divide evenly between the paper cases before rapping the tin on a work surface to help settle the batter.

- Bake for 15–18 minutes until risen and a toothpick inserted into the centre comes out clean.

- Transfer the cakes to a wire rack and leave to cool.

- Beat the butter with the icing sugar and food dye until smooth.

- Spread the buttercream on top of the cakes, then sprinkle with blueberries and sugar.

TOP TIP

Decorate the cakes with the finely grated zest of an orange.

Painted Rose Cupcakes

MAKES 12

PREPARATION TIME 1 HOUR

COOKING TIME 12–15 MINUTES

INGREDIENTS

110 g / 4 oz / 1 cup self-raising flour, sifted

110 g / 4 oz / ½ cup caster (superfine) sugar

110 g / 4 oz / ½ cup butter, softened

2 large eggs

1 tsp rosewater

TO DECORATE

100 g / 3 ½ oz ready-to-roll fondant icing

pink, purple and green food dye

110 g / 4 oz / ½ cup butter, softened

225 g / 8 oz / 2 cups icing (confectioners')
sugar, plus extra for dusting

1 tbsp milk

1 tsp rosewater

METHOD

- Roll out the fondant icing and cut out
  12 circles. Leave to dry and harden on a
  flat surface overnight.

- Preheat the oven to 190°C (170°C fan) /
  375F / gas 5 and line a 12-hole cupcake tin
  with paper cases.

- Combine the flour, sugar, butter, eggs and
  rosewater in a bowl and whisk together for
  2 minutes or until smooth.

- Divide the mixture between the cake
  cases then transfer the tin to the oven
  and bake for 10–15 minutes. Test with a
  wooden toothpick inserted into the centre;
  if it comes out clean, the cakes are done.
  Transfer the cakes to a wire rack and leave
  to cool completely.

- To make the buttercream, beat the butter
  until smooth then beat in the icing sugar.
  Use a whisk to incorporate the milk and
  rosewater, then whisk for 2 minutes or
  until well whipped. Spread the icing over
  the cakes.

- Use a fine paintbrush to paint the rose
  design onto the hardened fondant plaques,
  then transfer them to the top of the cakes.

TOP TIP

Try adding ground
almonds to the cake
mixture for a nutty
alternative.

Orange Blossom Cupcakes

MAKES 12

PREPARATION TIME 30 MINUTES

COOKING TIME 15–18 MINUTES

INGREDIENTS

110 g / 4 oz / ⅔ cup self-raising flour, sifted

110 g / 4 oz / ½ cup margarine

110 g / 4 oz / ½ cup caster (superfine) sugar

1 tsp orange flower water

2 large eggs

a pinch of salt

TO DECORATE

200 g / 7 oz / 1 cup butter, softened

400 g / 14 oz / 4 cups icing (confectioners')
    sugar

1 tsp orange flower water

a few drops of orange food dye

12 sugar paste flowers

METHOD

- Preheat the oven to 190°C (170°C fan) / 375F / gas 5 and line a 12-hole cupcake tin with paper cases.

- Combine the cake ingredients and whisk together until smooth.

- Divide the mixture between the cases and bake for 15–20 minutes. Test with a wooden toothpick inserted into the centre; if it comes out clean, the cakes are done.

- Transfer the cakes to a wire rack and leave to cool.

- Beat the butter with the icing sugar, orange flower water and food dye until smooth.

- Pipe the icing onto the cakes and garnish each one with a flower.

TOP TIP

These cakes look beautiful decorated with fresh orange blossoms.

Dark Chocolate Delight Cupcakes

MAKES 12

PREPARATION TIME 45 MINUTES

COOKING TIME 20 MINUTES

INGREDIENTS

125 g / 4 ½ oz / ½ cup unsalted butter, softened

125 g / 4 ½ oz / ½ cup caster (superfine) sugar

2 medium eggs, room temperature

½ tsp vanilla extract

125 g / 4 ½ oz / ¾ cup self-raising flour

2 tbsp cocoa

45 ml / 1 ½ fl. oz / ¼ cup milk

TO DECORATE

125 g / 4 ½ oz / ½ cup unsalted butter, softened

300 g / 10 ½ oz / 2 ½ cups icing (confectioners') sugar

½ tsp vanilla extract

½ tbsp milk

50 g / 2 oz / ¼ cup chocolate, grated

METHOD

- Preheat the oven to 180°C (160°C fan) / 350F / gas 4 and line a cupcake tin with paper cases.

- Cream the butter and sugar together until pale and fluffy.

- Gradually mix in the eggs and vanilla extract.

- Gently mix in the flour and cocoa, adding the milk.

- Spoon the cupcake mix into each paper case.

- Bake for 18–20 minutes. Test with a wooden toothpick inserted into the centre; if it comes out clean, the cakes are done.

- Place on a wire rack to cool.

- To make the buttercream, beat the butter with a whisk until soft then gradually beat in the icing sugar, vanilla and milk.

- Spoon the icing into a piping bag fitted with a star nozzle and pipe a swirl onto each cupcake. Decorate with grated chocolate.

TOP TIP

Try adding a few drops of peppermint essence to the cake mixture and icing.

Coconut and Strawberry Cupcakes

MAKES 12

PREPARATION TIME 40 MINUTES

COOKING TIME 15–20 MINUTES

INGREDIENTS

110 g / 4 oz / ⅔ cup self-raising flour, sifted

110 g / 4 oz / ½ cup caster (superfine) sugar

110 g / 4 oz / ½ cup butter, softened

3 tbsp desiccated coconut

2 tbsp milk

2 large eggs

TO DECORATE

3 tbsp strawberry jam (jelly)

100 g / 3 ½ oz / ½ cup butter, softened

200 g / 7 oz / 2 cups icing (confectioners')
    sugar

100 g / 3 ½ oz / 1 cup desiccated coconut

12 strawberries

METHOD

- Preheat the oven to 190°C (170°C fan) / 375F / gas 5 and line a 12-hole cupcake tin with paper cases.

- Measure the cake ingredients into a bowl then whisk together for 3 minutes or until smooth and light. Divide the mixture between the paper cases, then transfer the tin to the oven and bake for 15–20 minutes.

- Test the cakes with a toothpick; if it comes out clean, the cakes are done. Leave to cool completely.

- Cut a cone out of the centre of each cake and fill with strawberry jam before replacing the cake plugs.

- Whisk the butter until smooth, then gradually incorporate the icing sugar and whisk until smooth.

- Spread the buttercream onto the cakes, then dip the tops in desiccated coconut to coat.

- Top each cake with a fresh strawberry.

TOP TIP

Use coconut milk in place of the milk for natural sweetness.

Chocolate Star Cupcakes

MAKES 12

PREPARATION TIME 40 MINUTES

COOKING TIME 20–25 MINUTES

INGREDIENTS

75 g / 3 oz / ½ cup dark chocolate

200 g / 7 oz / 1 cup butter, unsalted, softened

225 g / 8 oz / 1 cup caster (superfine) sugar

3 eggs

½ tsp baking powder

175 g / 6 oz / 1 ½ cups plain (all purpose)
    flour

25 g / 1 oz / ¼ cup cocoa powder

50 g / 2 oz / ½ cup dark chocolate chips

TO DECORATE

25 g / 1 oz / ⅙ cup dark chocolate, melted

50 g / 2 oz / ¼ cup unsalted butter, softened

100 g / 3 ½ oz / 1 cup icing (confectioners')
    sugar

½ tsp vanilla extract

12 chocolate stars

METHOD

- Preheat the oven to 200°C (180°C fan) /
  400F / gas 6 and line a cupcake tin with
  paper cases.

- In a large saucepan, melt the chocolate
  and butter over medium heat, stirring to
  prevent burning. Allow this to cool for a
  few minutes.

- Stir in the sugar until well mixed. Add
  the eggs, one at a time, until you have a
  smooth batter. Sift the baking powder,
  flour and cocoa into the batter and mix
  until smooth. Fold in the chocolate chips.

- Spoon the cupcake mixture into the
  paper cases.

- Bake for 20–25 minutes. Test with a
  wooden toothpick inserted into the centre;
  if it comes out clean, the cakes are done.

- Place on a wire rack to cool.

- For the icing, beat together the melted
  chocolate, butter, icing sugar and vanilla
  extract until smooth and well whipped.

- Spoon into a piping bag fitted with a plain
  nozzle and pipe small swirls on the top of
  each cake. Decorate with chocolate stars.

TOP TIP

Sprinkle the cakes with
edible glitter for extra
star power.

Raspberry Truffle Cupcakes

MAKES 12

PREPARATION TIME 30 MINUTES

COOKING TIME 15–18 MINUTES

INGREDIENTS

110 g / 4 oz / ⅔ cup self-raising flour, sifted

110 g / 4 oz / ½ cup margarine, softened

110 g / 4 oz / ½ cup caster (superfine) sugar

1 tsp vanilla extract

2 large eggs

a pinch of salt

TO DECORATE

100 g / 3 ½ oz / ½ cup butter, softened

200 g / 7 oz / 2 cups golden icing (confectioners') sugar

a few drops of pink food dye

1 tbsp whole milk

TO GARNISH

12 raspberries

METHOD

- Preheat the oven to 180°C (160°C fan) / 350F / gas 4 and line a 12-hole cupcake tin with 12 cupcake cases.

- Beat together all the ingredients for the batter in a mixing bowl for 2 minutes until smooth and creamy.

- Divide evenly between the paper cases before rapping the tin on a work surface to help settle the batter.

- Bake for 15–18 minutes until risen; test with a wooden toothpick into the centre; if it comes out clean, the cakes are done.

- Remove to a wire rack to cool as you prepare the buttercream.

- Beat the softened butter with the icing sugar, food dye and milk in a mixing bowl until smooth and creamy.

- Spoon into a piping bag fitted with a star-shaped nozzle and pipe in swirls on top of the cupcakes.

- Garnish the tops with a raspberry before serving.

TOP TIP

Add the seeds from a vanilla pod to the buttercream for sweetness.

Pink Crown Raspberry Cupcakes

MAKES 12

PREPARATION TIME 30 MINUTES

COOKING TIME 15–18 MINUTES

INGREDIENTS

110 g / 4 oz / ⅔ cup self-raising flour, sifted
110 g / 4 oz / ½ cup margarine, softened
110 g / 4 oz / ½ cup caster (superfine) sugar
1 tsp vanilla extract
2 large eggs
a pinch of salt

TO DECORATE

100 g / 3 ½ oz / ½ cup butter, softened
200 g / 7 oz / 2 cups icing (confectioners')
    sugar
2 tbsp Framboise liqueur
200 g / 7 oz / 2 cups raspberries

METHOD

- Preheat the oven to 180°C (160°C fan) / 350F / gas 4 and line a 12-hole cupcake tin with 12 cupcake cases.

- Beat together all the ingredients for the batter in a mixing bowl for 2 minutes until smooth and creamy.

- Divide evenly between the paper cases before rapping the tin on a work surface to help settle the batter.

- Bake for 15–18 minutes until risen; test with a wooden toothpick inserted into the centre; if it comes out clean, the cakes are done.

- Remove to a wire rack to cool as you prepare the buttercream.

- Beat the softened butter in a mixing bowl for 3-4 minutes until pale.

- Add the icing sugar and the Framboise and beat again until smooth.

- Spoon into a piping bag fitted with a star-shaped nozzle and pipe a rosette on top of each cupcake.

- Garnish the perimeter with raspberries before serving.

TOP TIP

Add 3 tbsp of raspberry syrup to the cake mixture for added sweetness.

Hot Chocolate Cupcakes

MAKES 6

PREPARATION TIME 20 MINUTES

COOKING TIME 20—25 MINUTES

INGREDIENTS

110 g / 4 oz / ⅔ cup self-raising flour, sifted

110 g / 4 oz / ½ cup caster (superfine) sugar

110 g / 4 oz / ½ cup butter, softened

2 large eggs

2 tbsp unsweetened cocoa powder

TO DECORATE

400 ml / 14 fl. oz / 1 ⅔ cups double (heavy) cream

6 mint chocolate matchmakers

unsweetened cocoa powder for sprinkling

METHOD

- Preheat the oven to 190°C (170°C fan) / 375F / gas 5 and butter 6 ovenproof mugs.

- Whisk the cake ingredients together for 3 minutes or until smooth. Divide the mixture between the mugs and bake for 20–25 minutes.

- Test with a wooden toothpick inserted into the centre; if it comes out clean, the cakes are done.

- Whisk the cream until it holds its shape, then spoon it on top of the warm cakes.

- Cut the matchmakers in half and add two halves to each cake with a sprinkle of cocoa powder.

- Serve immediately.

TOP TIP

Top the cakes with mini marshmallows for a extra of luxury.

Toffee Fudge Cupcakes

MAKES 12

PREPARATION TIME 30 MINUTES

COOKING TIME 15–20 MINUTES

INGREDIENTS

110 g / 4 oz / ⅔ cup self-raising flour, sifted

110 g / 4 oz / ½ cup caster (superfine) sugar

110 g / 4 oz / ½ cup butter, softened

2 large eggs

2 tbsp unsweetened cocoa powder

75 g / 2 ½ oz / ½ cup fudge pieces

TO DECORATE

100 g / 3 ½ oz / ½ cup butter, softened

200 g / 7 oz / 2 cups icing (confectioners') sugar

2 tbsp milk

2 tbsp unsweetened cocoa powder

2 tbsp toffee sauce

75 g / 2 ½ oz / ½ cup fudge pieces

bronze crunch sprinkles

METHOD

- Preheat the oven to 190°C (170°C fan) / 375F / gas 5 and line a 12-hole cupcake tin with paper cases.

- Whisk the cake ingredients together for 3 minutes or until smooth. Divide the mixture between the cases and bake for 15–20 minutes.

- Test with a wooden toothpick inserted into the centre; if it comes out clean, the cakes are done. Leave to cool completely.

- Beat the butter until smooth, then gradually whisk in the icing sugar, milk and cocoa powder.

- Spoon the buttercream into a piping bag fitted with a large star nozzle and pipe a big swirl onto the cupcakes.

- Drizzle the cakes with toffee sauce, then sprinkle with fudge pieces and bronze crunch sprinkles.

TOP TIP

Remove a cone of cake and fill the centres with dulce de leche before icing.

Mochaccino Cupcakes

MAKES 12

PREPARATION TIME 45 MINUTES

COOKING TIME 15–18 MINUTES

INGREDIENTS

110 g / 4 oz / ⅔ cup self-raising flour, sifted

110 g / 4 oz / ½ cup margarine

110 g / 4 oz / ½ cup caster (superfine) sugar

55 g / 2 oz / ⅓ cup cocoa powder

55 ml / 2 fl. oz / ¼ cup whole milk

2 large eggs

a pinch of salt

TO DECORATE

100 g / 3 ½ oz / ½ cup butter, softened

200 g / 7 oz / 2 cups icing (confectioners')
   sugar

1 tsp strong instant espresso powder

55 g / 2 oz / ⅓ cup dark chocolate, melted

METHOD

- Preheat the oven to 180°C (160°C fan) / 350F / gas 4 and line a 12-hole cupcake tin with 12 cupcake cases.

- Beat together all the ingredients for the batter apart from the milk in a mixing bowl for 2 minutes.

- Add the milk and beat again for a further minute.

- Divide evenly between the paper cases before rapping the tin on a work surface to help settle the batter.

- Bake for 15–18 minutes until risen. Test with a wooden toothpick inserted into the centre; if it comes out clean, the cakes are done.

- Remove to a wire rack to cool.

- Beat the softened butter with the icing sugar in a mixing bowl until smooth.

- Mix together the espresso powder with 1 tbsp boiling water until smooth, then beat into the buttercream.

- Spoon into a piping bag fitted with a straight-sided nozzle and pipe a mound on top of each cupcake.

- Pipe small blobs of chocolate on top of the buttercream.

TOP TIP

Add 1 tsp of instant espresso powder to the cake mixture.

Violet Tip Cupcakes

MAKES 12

PREPARATION TIME 35 MINUTES

COOKING TIME 15–20 MINUTES

INGREDIENTS

110 g / 4 oz / ⅔ cup self-raising flour, sifted

110 g / 4 oz / ½ cup margarine, softened

110 g / 4 oz / ½ cup caster (superfine) sugar

1 tsp vanilla extract

2 large eggs

1 pinch of salt

TO DECORATE

100 g / 3 ½ oz / ½ cup unsalted butter,
    softened

200 g / 7 oz / 2 cups icing (confectioners')
    sugar

1 tsp vanilla extract

a few drops of purple food dye

2 drops of violet essence

METHOD

- Preheat the oven to 190°C (170°C fan) / 375F / gas 5 and line a 12-hole cupcake tin with paper cases.

- Combine the cake ingredients and whisk together for 2 minutes.

- Divide the mixture between the cases and bake for 15–20 minutes.

- Test with a wooden toothpick inserted into the centre; if it comes out clean, the cakes are done.

- Transfer the cakes to a wire rack and leave to cool.

- Beat the butter with the icing sugar and vanilla extract until smooth.

- Pipe two thirds of the icing onto the cakes in small rosettes.

- Add a few drops of food dye and violet essence to the remaining icing, then pipe purple rosettes on top.

TOP TIP

Add a few drops of violet essence to the cake mixture.

Chocolate Marshmallow Cupcakes

MAKES 12

PREPARATION TIME 45 MINUTES

COOKING TIME 15–20 MINUTES

INGREDIENTS

110 g / 4 oz / ⅔ cup self-raising flour, sifted
110 g / 4 oz / ½ cup caster (superfine) sugar
110 g / 4 oz / ½ cup butter, softened
2 large eggs
2 tbsp unsweetened cocoa powder

TO DECORATE

100 g / 3 ½ oz / ½ cup butter, softened
200 g / 7 oz / 2 cups icing (confectioners')
    sugar
1 tbsp milk
2 tbsp unsweetened cocoa powder
150 g / 5 ½ oz / 2 ½ cups mini marshmallows
30 g / 1 oz / ¼ cup red sweets
2 tbsp chocolate shavings

METHOD

- Preheat the oven to 190°C (170°C fan) / 375F / gas 5 and line a 12-hole cupcake tin with paper cases.

- Whisk the cake ingredients together for 3 minutes or until smooth. Divide the mixture between the cases and bake for 15–20 minutes.

- Test with a wooden toothpick inserted into the centre; if it comes out clean, the cakes are done. Leave to cool completely.

- Beat the butter until smooth, then gradually whisk in the icing sugar, milk and cocoa powder.

- Spoon the buttercream into a piping bag fitted with a large star nozzle and pipe a big rosette onto each cupcake.

- Top the cakes with the marshmallows, red sweets and a sprinkle of chocolate shavings.

TOP TIP

For a quick and easy icing, use a jar of marshmallow fluff.

Soured Cream Cupcakes

MAKES 12

PREPARATION TIME 40 MINUTES

COOKING TIME 15–18 MINUTES

INGREDIENTS

110 g / 4 oz / ⅔ cup self-raising flour, sifted
110 g / 4 oz / ½ cup margarine, softened
110 g / 4 oz / ½ cup caster (superfine) sugar
1 tsp vanilla extract
2 large eggs
a pinch of salt

TO DECORATE

30 g / 1 oz / ¼ cup butter, softened
75 ml / 2 ½ fl. oz / ⅓ cup soured cream
300 g / 10 ½ oz / 3 cups icing (confectioners')
     sugar
1 tsp vanilla extract
a few drops violet food dye

METHOD

- Preheat the oven to 180°C (160°C fan) / 350F / gas 4 and line a 12-hole cupcake tin with 12 cupcake cases.

- Beat together all the ingredients for the batter in a mixing bowl for 2 minutes until smooth and creamy.

- Divide evenly between the paper cases.

- Bake for 15–18 minutes until risen. Test with a wooden toothpick inserted into the centre; if it comes out clean, the cakes are done. Leave to cool.

- Beat the butter and soured cream in a mixing bowl before adding the icing sugar and vanilla extract.

- Spoon most of the icing into a piping bag fitted with a star-shaped nozzle.

- Add drops of the food dye to the remaining icing, beating well until purple.

- Spoon into a small piping bag fitted with a small straight-sided nozzle.

- Pipe the plain vanilla icing in a swirl on top of the cupcakes before dotting with beads of purple icing.

TOP TIP
Replace the vanilla with the finely grated zest of a lemon.

Passion Fruit Cupcakes

MAKES 12
PREPARATION TIME 50 MINUTES
COOKING TIME 15–20 MINUTES

INGREDIENTS

110 g / 4 oz / ⅔ cup self-raising flour, sifted

110 g / 4 oz / ½ cup caster (superfine) sugar

110 g / 4 oz / ½ cup butter, softened

3 passion fruit, pulp sieved and seeds removed

2 large eggs

TO DECORATE

400 ml / 14 fl. oz / 1 ⅔ cups double (heavy) cream

3 tbsp icing (confectioners') sugar

3 passion fruit

METHOD

- Preheat the oven to 190°C (170°C fan) / 375F / gas 5 and line a 12-hole cupcake tin with paper cases.

- Whisk the cake ingredients together until smooth and light. Divide the mixture between the paper cases and bake for 15–20 minutes or until a toothpick inserted into the centre comes out clean. Leave to cool completely.

- Whip the cream with the icing sugar until it holds its shape, then pipe a big swirl onto each cake.

- Cut open the passion fruit, then spoon the pulp and seeds over the cakes.

TOP TIP
Try stirring a handful of dark chocolate chips through the cake mixture.

Dairy-free Vanilla Cupcakes

MAKES 12

PREPARATION TIME 45 MINUTES

COOKING TIME 15–20 MINUTES

INGREDIENTS

110 g / 4 oz / ⅔ cup self-raising flour, sifted
110 g / 4 oz / ½ cup caster (superfine) sugar
110 g / 4 oz / ½ cup sunflower margarine
1 tsp vanilla extract
2 large eggs

TO DECORATE

100 g / 3 ½ oz / ½ cup sunflower margarine
200 g / 7 oz / 2 cups icing (confectioners')
      sugar
1 tsp vanilla extract
edible silver balls

METHOD

- Preheat the oven to 190°C (170°C fan) / 375F / gas 5 and line a 12-hole cupcake tin with paper cases.

- Whisk the cake ingredients together until smooth and light. Divide the mixture between the paper cases and bake for 15–20 minutes or until a toothpick inserted into the centre comes out clean. Leave to cool completely.

- Whisk the margarine, icing sugar and vanilla extract together until smooth then whip for 2 minutes.

- Spoon the icing into a piping bag fitted with a large star nozzle and pipe a swirl onto each cake. Scatter over the silver balls.

TOP TIP
Try decorating the cakes with grated white chocolate.

Blackberries and Cream Cupcakes

MAKES 12

PREPARATION TIME 40 MINUTES

COOKING TIME 15–20 MINUTES

INGREDIENTS

110 g / 4 oz / ⅔ cup self-raising flour, sifted

110 g / 4 oz / ½ cup caster (superfine) sugar

110 g / 4 oz / ½ cup butter, softened

1 tsp finely grated orange zest

2 large eggs

12 blackberries

TO DECORATE

400 ml / 14 fl. oz / 1 ⅔ cups double (heavy) cream

3 tbsp blackberry syrup

12 blackberries

METHOD

- Preheat the oven to 190°C (170°C fan) / 375F / gas 5 and line a 12-hole cupcake tin with paper cases.

- Measure the cake ingredients into a bowl then whisk together for 3 minutes or until smooth and light.

- Divide the mixture between the paper cases, then press a blackberry into the centre of each one. Bake the cakes for 15–20 minutes or until a skewer inserted into the centre comes out clean. Leave to cool completely.

- Whip the cream until it holds its shape, then pipe a swirl on top of each cake.

- Drizzle the cakes with the blackberry syrup and top each one with a blackberry.

TOP TIP

Top the cakes with a sprinkle of orange zest for a zesty finish.

Chocolate Cookies and Cream Cupcakes

MAKES 12

PREPARATION TIME **30 MINUTES**

COOKING TIME **15–18 MINUTES**

INGREDIENTS

110 g / 4 oz / ⅔ cup self-raising flour, sifted

110 g / 4 oz / ½ cup margarine, softened

110 g / 4 oz / ½ cup caster (superfine) sugar

25 g / 2 oz / ⅓ cup cocoa powder

2 tbsp whole milk

2 large eggs

1 pinch of salt

TO DECORATE

100 g / 3 ½ oz / ½ cup unsalted butter, softened

200 g / 7 oz / 2 cups icing (confectioners') sugar

1 chocolate biscuit, crushed

6 chocolate biscuits, lightly crushed

METHOD

- Preheat the oven to 180°C (160°C fan) / 350F / gas 4 and line a 12-hole cupcake tin with 12 cupcake cases.

- Beat together all the ingredients for the batter apart from the milk in a mixing bowl for 2 minutes until smooth and creamy.

- Add the milk and beat again for a further minute.

- Divide evenly between the paper cases before rapping the tin on a work surface to help settle the batter.

- Bake for 15–18 minutes until risen; test with a wooden toothpick inserted into the centre; if it comes out clean, the cakes are done.

- Remove to a wire rack to cool as you prepare the buttercream.

- Beat the softened butter for 3–4 minutes in a mixing bowl until pale and creamy.

- Add the icing sugar and beat again until smooth before folding through the crushed chocolate biscuit.

- Spread the tops of the cupcakes with the icing before garnishing the top with lightly crushed chocolate biscuits.

TOP TIP
Try using chocolate chip cookies in place of the biscuits.

Pomegranate and Rose Water Cupcakes

MAKES 12
PREPARATION TIME 40 MINUTES
COOKING TIME 15–20 MINUTES

INGREDIENTS

110 g / 4 oz / ⅔ cup self-raising flour, sifted

110 g / 4 oz / ½ cup caster (superfine) sugar

110 g / 4 oz / ½ cup butter, softened

1 tbsp rose water

2 large eggs

TO DECORATE

400 ml / 14 fl. oz / 1 ⅔ cups double (heavy) cream

2 tbsp rose water

½ pomegranate

METHOD

- Preheat the oven to 190°C (170°C fan) / 375F / gas 5 and line a 12-hole cupcake tin with paper cases.

- Measure the cake ingredients into a bowl then whisk together for 3 minutes or until smooth and light. Divide the mixture between the paper cases, then transfer the tin to the oven and bake for 15–20 minutes.

- Test the cakes with a toothpick inserted into the centre; if it comes out clean, the cakes are done. Transfer the cakes to a wire rack and leave to cool completely.

- Whip the cream with the rose water until it holds its shape, then spread it onto the cakes.

- Hold the pomegranate half over a bowl and hit the back with a wooden spoon to release the seeds. Discard any bitter white pith, then sprinkle the seeds over the cakes.

TOP TIP
These cakes also look great garnished with fresh or dried rose petals.

Ginger Cream Cupcakes

MAKES 12

PREPARATION TIME 40 MINUTES

COOKING TIME 15–20 MINUTES

INGREDIENTS

110 g / 4 oz / ⅔ cup self-raising flour, sifted
110 g / 4 oz / ½ cup caster (superfine) sugar
110 g / 4 oz / ½ cup butter, softened
large eggs
tsp ground ginger
5 g / 2 ½ oz / ½ cup stem ginger in syrup,
    finely chopped

TO DECORATE

00 ml / 14 fl. oz / 1 ⅔ cups double (heavy)
    cream
tbsp syrup from the stem ginger jar
0 g / 1 oz / ¼ cup stem ginger in syrup,
    chopped

METHOD

- Preheat the oven to 190°C (170°C fan) / 375F / gas 5 and line a 12-hole cupcake tin with paper cases.

- Measure the cake ingredients into a bowl then whisk together for 3 minutes or until smooth and light.

- Divide the mixture between the paper cases and bake for 15–20 minutes or until a skewer inserted into the centre comes out clean. Leave to cool completely.

- Whip the cream with the ginger syrup until it holds its shape, then pipe a swirl on top of each cake.

- Sprinkle the cakes with the stem ginger pieces.

TOP TIP

Spoon a little syrup from the ginger jar over the finished cakes.

Very Cherry Cupcakes

MAKES 12

PREPARATION TIME 40 MINUTES

COOKING TIME 15–20 MINUTES

INGREDIENTS

110 g / 4 oz / ⅔ cup self-raising flour, sifted

110 g / 4 oz / ½ cup caster (superfine) sugar

110 g / 4 oz / ½ cup butter, softened

2 tbsp cherry syrup

2 large eggs

50 g / 1 ¾ oz / ¼ cup glacé cherries, chopped

TO DECORATE

100 g / 3 ½ oz / ½ cup butter, softened

200 g / 7 oz / 2 cups icing (confectioners')
     sugar

2 tbsp cherry syrup

24 glacé cherries

METHOD

- Preheat the oven to 190°C (170°C fan) / 375F / gas 5 and line a 12-hole cupcake tin with paper cases.

- Measure the cake ingredients into a bowl then whisk together for 3 minutes or until smooth and light. Divide the mixture between the paper cases and bake for 15–20 minutes.

- Test the cakes with a toothpick inserted into the centre; if it comes out clean, the cakes are done. Transfer the cakes to a wire rack and leave to cool completely.

- Whisk the butter until smooth, then gradually incorporate the icing sugar and cherry syrup. Whisk for 2 minutes or until light and fluffy.

- Spread the buttercream onto the cakes and top each one with a whole glacé cherry. Cut the remaining cherries into small pieces and dot them around the outside.

TOP TIP

These cakes look great garnished with whole fresh cherries when in season.

Rum and Raisin Cupcakes

MAKES 12

PREPARATION TIME 35 MINUTES

COOKING TIME 15–20 MINUTES

INGREDIENTS

100 g / 3 ½ oz ½ cup raisins

75 ml / 2 ½ fl. oz / ⅓ cup dark rum

110 g / 4 oz / ⅔ cup self-raising flour, sifted

110 g / 4 oz / ½ cup caster (superfine) sugar

110 g / 4 oz / ½ cup butter, softened

2 large eggs

TO DECORATE

400 ml / 14 fl. oz / 1 ⅔ cups double (heavy) cream

2 tbsp runny honey

METHOD

- Mix the raisins with the rum then cover and leave to macerate overnight.

- Preheat the oven to 190°C (170°C fan) / 375F / gas 5 and line a 12-hole cupcake tin with paper cases.

- Beat together the flour, sugar, butter and eggs with 50 g / 2 oz / ¼ cup of the raisins and 1 tbsp of the soaking liquor. Divide the mixture between the paper cases and bake for 15–20 minutes or until a skewer inserted into the centre comes out clean. Leave to cool completely.

- Whip the cream until it holds its shape, then pipe a swirl on top of each cake.

- Stir the honey into the rest of the rum and raisin mixture, then spoon it over the cakes.

TOP TIP

Try dried apricot pieces and brandy in place of the raisins and rum.

Raspberry and Marzipan Cupcakes

MAKES 12

PREPARATION TIME 50 MINUTES

COOKING TIME 15–20 MINUTES

INGREDIENTS

110 g / 4 oz / ⅔ cup self-raising flour, sifted

110 g / 4 oz / ½ cup caster (superfine) sugar

110 g / 4 oz / ½ cup butter, softened

1 tsp almond extract

2 large eggs

TO DECORATE

3 tbsp raspberry jam (jelly)

icing (confectioners') sugar to dust

300 g / 10 ½ oz / 1 ⅓ cups white marzipan

3 amaretti biscuits

12 raspberries

METHOD

- Preheat the oven to 190°C (170°C fan) / 375F / gas 5 and line a 12-hole cupcake tin with paper cases.

- Whisk the cake ingredients together for 3 minutes or until smooth. Divide the mixture between the paper cases and bake for 15–20 minutes.

- Test the cakes with a toothpick inserted into the centre; if it comes out clean, the cakes are done. Leave to cool completely.

- Cut a cone out of the centre of each cake and fill with the jam.

- Dust the work surface with icing sugar, then roll out the marzipan and cut out 12 thick discs. Transfer them to the top of the cakes and crumble over the amaretti biscuits. Top each cake with a raspberry.

TOP TIP

Fold fresh raspberries through the cake mixture for natural goodness.

Novelty

Walnut Cream Cupcakes

MAKES 12

PREPARATION TIME 40 MINUTES

COOKING TIME 15–20 MINUTES

INGREDIENTS

110 g / 4 oz / ⅔ cup self-raising flour, sifted

110 g / 4 oz / ½ cup caster (superfine) sugar

110 g / 4 oz / ½ cup butter, softened

2 large eggs

75 g / 2 ½ oz / ½ cup walnut pieces

TO DECORATE

400 ml / 14 fl. oz / 1 ⅔ cups double (heavy) cream

12 walnut halves

METHOD

- Preheat the oven to 190°C (170°C fan) / 375F / gas 5 and line a 12-hole cupcake tin with paper cases.

- Measure the cake ingredients into a bowl then whisk together for 3 minutes or until smooth and light.

- Divide the mixture between the paper cases and bake for 15–20 minutes or until a skewer inserted into the centre comes out clean. Leave to cool completely.

- Whip the cream until it holds its shape, then pipe a swirl on top of each cake and top with a walnut half.

- Sprinkle the cakes with walnut pieces and top each one with a walnut half.

TOP TIP
Add a few drops of almond extract for an extra nutty flavour.

Hedgehog Cupcakes

MAKES 12

PREPARATION TIME 1 HOUR 30 MINUTES

COOKING TIME 15–20 MINUTES

INGREDIENTS

- 0 g / 4 oz / ⅔ cup self-raising flour, sifted
- 0 g / 4 oz / ½ cup caster (superfine) sugar
- 0 g / 4 oz / ½ cup butter, softened
- large eggs
- tbsp unsweetened cocoa powder

DECORATE

- 0 g / 3 ½ oz / ½ cup butter, softened
- 0 g / 7 oz / 2 cups icing (confectioners') sugar
- own food dye
- 0 g / 3 ½ oz / ⅓ cup brown ready-to-roll fondant icing
- 0 g / 1 oz white ready-to-roll fondant icing
- g / 1 oz green ready-to-roll fondant icing

METHOD

- Preheat the oven to 190°C (170°C fan) / 375F / gas 5 and line a 12-hole cupcake tin with paper cases.

- Combine the cake ingredients and whisk until smooth.

- Divide the mixture between the cases and bake for 15–20 minutes or until a toothpick inserted into the centre comes out clean.

- Transfer the cakes to a wire rack and leave to cool.

- Beat the butter with the icing sugar and brown food dye then pipe it on top of the cakes.

- Shape three quarters of the brown fondant into 12 ovals then use a pair of scissors to snip the surface into spikes.

- Use the rest of the brown fondant to make the faces and the white fondant to make the eyes.

- Make 12 leaves from the green fondant and assemble the hedgehogs on top of the cakes.

TOP TIP
Use the same snipping technique to make pinecones and fir trees.

Birdcage Cupcakes

MAKES 12

PREPARATION TIME 1 HOUR 15 MINUTES

COOKING TIME 15–20 MINUTES

INGREDIENTS

110 g / 4 oz / ⅔ cup self-raising flour, sifted
110 g / 4 oz / ½ cup caster (superfine) sugar
110 g / 4 oz / ½ cup butter, softened
2 large eggs
1 tsp vanilla extract

TO DECORATE

100 g / 3 ½ oz / ½ cup butter, softened
200 g / 7 oz / 2 cups icing (confectioners')
   sugar
½ tsp vanilla extract
200 g / 7 oz / ½ cup ready-to-roll fondant
   icing
pink and brown food dye
12 small sugar flowers
12 sugar doves

METHOD

- Preheat the oven to 190°C (170°C fan) / 375F / gas 5 and line a 12-hole cupcake tin with paper cases.

- Combine the cake ingredients and whisk until smooth.

- Divide the mixture between the cases and bake for 15–20 minutes or until a toothpick inserted into the centre comes out clean.

- Transfer the cakes to a wire rack and leave to cool.

- Beat the butter with the icing sugar and vanilla extract and spread three quarters of it over the cakes.

- Reserve a quarter of the fondant icing and dye the rest pale pink.

- Roll it out and cut out 12 circles the same diameter as the cakes, then wet the backs and attach to the cakes.

- Dye the fondant icing pale pink.

- Attach the flowers and doves to the cage while the icing is still wet.

TOP TIP
Use the same piping technique to create a flower basket for the top of the cakes.

Butterfly Cupcakes

MAKES 12

PREPARATION TIME 1 HOUR 10 MINUTES

COOKING TIME 15–20 MINUTES

SETTING TIME OVER NIGHT

INGREDIENTS

110 g / 4 oz / ⅔ cup self-raising flour, sifted

110 g / 4 oz / ½ cup caster (superfine) sugar

110 g / 4 oz / ½ cup butter, softened

2 large eggs

1 tbsp unsweetened cocoa powder

TO DECORATE

110 g / 4 oz / ⅓ cup ready-to-roll fondant icing

orange food dye powder

100 g / 3 ½ oz / ½ cup butter, softened

200 g / 7 oz / 2 cups icing (confectioners') sugar

½ tsp vanilla extract

METHOD

- Fold a piece of card in half to make a 'v' shape and lay the butterflies down the centre. Leave to set and harden overnight.

- Preheat the oven to 190°C (170°C fan) / 375F / gas 5 and line a 12-hole cupcake tin with paper cases.

- Combine the flour, sugar, butter, eggs and cocoa powder in a bowl and whisk for 2 minutes or until smooth. Divide the mixture between the cases, then transfer the tin to the oven and bake for 15–20 minutes or until a toothpick inserted into the centre comes out clean.

- Transfer the cakes to a wire rack and leave to cool.

- Roll out the fondant icing and cut out 12 butterfly shapes.

- Put a little orange food dye powder in a plastic tray and add a few drops of water to make a paint.

- Paint the edge of the wings and the body onto the butterflies then add a spot to each wing.

- Beat the butter until smooth, then gradually whisk in the icing sugar, vanilla extract and a little of the orange food dye powder.

- Spoon the mixture into a piping bag, fitted with a large star nozzle. Starting in the centre, pipe the icing on in a spiral, keeping the piping bag completely vertical to produce a rose effect.

- Press a butterfly onto the side of each one.

Pumpkin Cupcakes

MAKES 12

PREPARATION TIME 1 HOUR

COOKING TIME 20–25 MINUTES

INGREDIENTS

175 g / 6 oz / 1 cup soft brown sugar

2 large eggs

150 ml / 5 fl. oz / ¾ cup sunflower oil

175 g / 6 oz / 1 ¼ cups wholemeal flour

3 tsp baking powder

2 tsp ground cinnamon, plus extra for
dusting

1 orange, zest finely grated

200 g / 7 oz / 1 cup pumpkin or butternut
squash, peeled and coarsely grated

TO DECORATE

110g / 4 oz / ⅓ cup ready-to-roll fondant
icing

orange and green food dye

100 g / 3 ½ oz / ½ cup unsalted butter,
softened

200 g / 7 oz / 2 cups icing (confectioners')
sugar

½ tsp vanilla extract

METHOD

- Preheat the oven to 190°C (170°C fan) /
375F / gas 5 and line a 12-hole cupcake
tin with paper cases.

- Whisk the sugar, eggs and oil together
for 3 minutes then fold in the flour,
baking powder and cinnamon, followed
by the orange zest and pumpkin.

- Divide the mixture between the paper
cases and bake for 20–25 minutes
or until a skewer inserted into the
centre comes out clean. Leave to cool
completely.

- Reserve a small piece of fondant and dye
the rest orange. Shape into pumpkins
and mark on the lines with a blunt
knife. Dye the reserved fondant green to
make the stalks.

- Whisk together the butter, icing sugar
and vanilla until well whipped. Transfer
two thirds to a separate bowl. Dye the
smaller amount orange.

- Pipe the plain buttercream in a large
pillow in the centre of each cake.
Dust with cinnamon. Pipe the orange
buttercream in a ring around the edge.
Top with a pumpkin.

TOP TIP

Add a touch of nutmeg
and ground ginger to
the cake mixture for
aromatic spice.

Sheep Cupcakes

MAKES 12

PREPARATION TIME 1 HOUR 30 MINUTES

COOKING TIME 15–20 MINUTES

INGREDIENTS

110 g / 4 oz / ⅔ cup self-raising flour, sifted

110 g / 4 oz / ½ cup caster (superfine) sugar

110 g / 4 oz / ½ cup butter, softened

2 large eggs

2 tbsp unsweetened cocoa powder

TO DECORATE

100 g / 3 ½ oz / ½ cup butter, softened

200 g / 7 oz / 2 cups icing (confectioners') sugar

½ tsp vanilla extract

green food dye

300 g / 10 ½ oz / 1 cup ready-to-roll fondant icing

pink and blue food dye

150 g / 5 ½ oz / 1 ½ cups mini marshmallows

METHOD

- Preheat the oven to 190°C (170°C fan) / 375F / gas 5 and line a 12-hole cupcake tin with paper cases.
- Combine the flour, sugar, butter, eggs and cocoa powder and whisk for 2 minutes. Divide the mixture between the cases, then bake for 15–20 minutes or until a toothpick inserted into the centre comes out clean.
- Transfer the cakes to a wire rack and leave to cool.
- Beat the butter until smooth, then gradually whisk in the icing sugar and vanilla extract.
- Dye the buttercream pale green and spread half of it over the surface of the cakes.
- Spoon the rest into a piping bag and pipe a ring of teardrops round the edge of each cake.
- Dye a third of the fondant icing pale pink. Shape it into 12 quail's egg shapes and 48 pea-sized balls.
- Flatten 24 of the pea-sized balls and pinch one end together to make the ears.
- Use a little of the white icing to make circles for the eyes. Paint the pupils in with blue food dye. Use a scalpel to score in the mouth details.
- Make 2 indentations in each head and insert the ears.
- Shape the white icing into 12 bodies and attach a head and 2 front feet to each one with a little water.
- Cut the mini marshmallows in half with scissors.
- Use the sticky side of the marshmallows to attach to the sheep, then transfer to the top of a cake.

White-choc Easter Cupcakes

MAKES 12

PREPARATION TIME 1 HOUR

COOKING TIME 15–20 MINUTES

INGREDIENTS

110 g / 4 oz / ⅔ cup self-raising flour, sifted

110 g / 4 oz / ½ cup caster (superfine) sugar

110 g / 4 oz / ½ cup butter, softened

2 large eggs

1 tsp vanilla extract

75 g / 2 ½ oz / ½ cup white chocolate, roughly
    chopped

TO DECORATE

100 g / 3 ½ oz / ½ cup butter

200 g / 7 oz / 2 cups icing (confectioners')
    sugar

4 tbsp white chocolate, melted

purple and white sugar sprinkles

36 chocolate mini eggs

METHOD

- Preheat the oven to 190°C (170°C fan) / 375F / gas 5 and line a 12-hole cupcake tin with paper cases.

- Combine the flour, sugar, butter, eggs and vanilla extract in a bowl and whisk together for 2 minutes or until smooth. Fold in the chocolate chunks then divide the mixture between the cases and bake for 15–20 minutes.

- Test with a wooden toothpick inserted into the centre; if it comes out clean, the cakes are done. Transfer the cakes to a wire rack and leave to cool completely.

- Beat the butter until smooth, then gradually whisk in the icing sugar and melted chocolate.

- Spoon the buttercream into a piping bag fitted with a large star nozzle and pipe a swirl onto each cake.

- Sprinkle the cakes with purple and white sugar sprinkles and top each one with 3 mini eggs.

TOP TIP
Sprinkle with cocoa powder before adding the eggs for a yummy finish.

Nice Cuppa Cupcakes

MAKES 12

PREPARATION TIME 1 HOUR 30 MINUTES

COOKING TIME 15–20 MINUTES

INGREDIENTS

110 g / 4 oz / ⅔ cup self-raising flour, sifted

110 g / 4 oz / ½ cup caster (superfine) sugar

110 g / 4 oz / ½ cup butter, softened

2 tsp instant tea powder

2 large eggs

TO DECORATE

110 g / 4 oz / ⅓ cup ready-to-roll fondant icing

red food dye pens

100 g / 3 ½ oz / ½ cup unsalted butter, softened

200 g / 7 oz / 2 cups icing (confectioners') sugar

½ tsp vanilla extract

METHOD

- Preheat the oven to 190°C (170°C fan) / 375F / gas 5 and line a 12-hole cupcake tin with paper cases.

- Whisk the cake ingredients together for 3 minutes. Divide the mixture between the paper cases and bake for 15–20 minutes.

- Test the cakes with a toothpick inserted into the centre; if it comes out clean, the cakes are done. Leave to cool completely.

- Beat the butter until smooth then beat in the icing sugar and vanilla until well whipped. Spread three quarters of the icing over the cupcakes.

- Dye the fondant icing red and roll out on a board. Cut out 12 teapot shapes and transfer to the tops of the cupcakes. Pipe on details with the remaining buttercream.

TOP TIP

These cakes also taste great with matcha green tea powder.

Ice Cream Cone Cupcakes

MAKES 12

PREPARATION TIME 45 MINUTES

COOKING TIME 12–18 MINUTES

INGREDIENTS

110 g / 4 oz / ⅔ cup self-raising flour, sifted

110 g / 4 oz / ½ cup caster (superfine) sugar

110 g / 4 oz / ½ cup butter, softened

2 large eggs

1 tsp vanilla extract

12 ice cream cones

TO DECORATE

100 g / 3 ½ oz / ½ cup butter, softened

200 g / 7 oz / 2 cups icing (confectioners')
    sugar

1 tbsp milk

1 tbsp hundreds and thousands

1 tbsp sugar stars

METHOD

- Preheat the oven to 190°C (170°C fan) / 375F / gas 5.

- Whisk the cake ingredients together for 3 minutes or until smooth. Divide the mixture between 12 ice cream cones, then stand them upright in a deep cake tin and bake for 12–18 minutes.

- Test with a wooden toothpick inserted into the centre; if it comes out clean, the cakes are done. Leave to cool completely.

- Beat the butter until smooth, then gradually whisk in the icing sugar and milk.

- Spoon the buttercream into a piping bag fitted with a large star nozzle and pipe a big swirl on top of each cone.

- Sprinkle with hundreds and thousands and sugar stars.

TOP TIP

Top each cake with a chocolate flake for a delicious treat.

Knitting Cupcakes

MAKES 12

PREPARATION TIME 1 HOUR 30 MINUTES

COOKING TIME 15–20 MINUTES

INGREDIENTS

110 g / 4 oz / ⅔ cup self-raising flour, sifted

110 g / 4 oz / ½ cup caster (superfine) sugar

110 g / 4 oz / ½ cup butter, softened

1 tsp vanilla extract

2 large eggs

TO DECORATE

225 g / 8 oz / 1 cup white ready-to-roll
    fondant icing

225 g / 8 oz / 1 cup purple ready-to-roll
    fondant icing

METHOD

- Model the knitting needles out of the white fondant and leave to harden overnight.

- The next day, preheat the oven to 190°C (170°C fan) / 375F / gas 5 and line a 12-hole cupcake tin with paper cases.

- Whisk the cake ingredients together then divide between the paper cases and bake for 15–20 minutes or until a toothpick inserted into the centre comes out clean. Leave to cool completely.

- Roll out half of the purple fondant and cut out 12 circles the same diameter as the top of the cakes. Brush the backs with water and smooth onto the cakes. Mark on the lines of the wool with a blunt knife.

- Roll the rest of the purple fondant into thin strands and build up the wool pattern.

- Cut the "knitting needles" in half and insert the ends into the icing so that it looks like they go all the way through.

TOP TIP

These delicious cakes make a great Mothers' Day gift.

Jam-filled Biscuit Cupcakes

MAKES 12

PREPARATION TIME 40 MINUTES

COOKING TIME 15—20 MINUTES

INGREDIENTS

110 g / 4 oz / ⅔ cup self-raising flour, sifted

110 g / 4 oz / ½ cup caster (superfine) sugar

110 g / 4 oz / ½ cup butter, softened

1 tsp vanilla extract

2 large eggs

TO DECORATE

100 g / 3 ½ oz / ½ cup strawberry jam (jelly)

400 ml / 14 fl. oz / 1 ⅔ cups double (heavy) cream

12 jam-filled mini biscuits

METHOD

- Preheat the oven to 190°C (170°C fan) / 375F / gas 5 and line a 12-hole cupcake tin with paper cases.

- Measure the cake ingredients into a bowl then whisk together for 3 minutes or until smooth and light.

- Divide the mixture between the paper cases, then transfer the tin to the oven and bake for 15–20 minutes or until a toothpick inserted into the centre comes out clean.

- Test the cakes with a toothpick; if it comes out clean, the cakes are done. Transfer the cakes to a wire rack and leave to cool completely.

- Cut a cone out of the centre of each cake and fill with a little strawberry jam, then replace the cones of cake.

- Whip the cream until it holds its shape, then pipe a swirl on top of each cake. Drizzle the cakes with the rest of the jam and top with the jam-filled biscuits.

TOP TIP
Stir 2 tbsp of strawberry jam through the cake mixture.

Blue Star Cupcakes

MAKES 12

PREPARATION TIME 50 MINUTES

COOKING TIME 10–15 MINUTES

INGREDIENTS

110 g / 4 oz / 1 cup self-raising flour, sifted

110 g / 4 oz / ½ cup caster (superfine) sugar

110 g / 4 oz / ½ cup butter, softened

2 large eggs

1 tsp vanilla extract

TO DECORATE

2 tbsp blueberry jam (jelly)

110 g / 4 oz / ½ cup butter, softened

225 g / 8 oz / 2 cups icing (confectioners')
   sugar, plus extra for dusting

1 tbsp milk

1 tsp vanilla extract

100 g / 3 ½ oz blue ready-to-roll fondant icing

METHOD

- Preheat the oven to 190°C (170°C fan) /
  375F / gas 5 and line a 12-hole cupcake tin
  with paper cases.

- Combine the flour, sugar, butter, eggs
  and vanilla extract in a bowl and whisk
  together for 2 minutes or until smooth.

- Divide the mixture between the cake
  cases then transfer the tin to the oven
  and bake for 10–15 minutes. Test with a
  wooden toothpick inserted into the centre;
  if it comes out clean, the cakes are done.
  Transfer the cakes to a wire rack and leave
  to cool completely.

- Cut a cone out of the centre of each cake
  and fill it with blueberry jam before
  placing the cake.

- To make the buttercream, beat the butter
  until smooth then beat in the icing sugar.
  Use a whisk to incorporate the milk and
  vanilla extract, then whisk for 2 minutes
  or until well whipped. Spoon the icing into
  a piping bag fitted with a large star nozzle
  and pipe a swirl onto each cake.

- Roll out the blue fondant icing and use
  a small star cutter to cut out the stars.
  Arrange them on top of the cakes.

TOP TIP

Replace the blueberry
jam with a spoonful
of fruit compote.

Four-leaf Clover Cupcakes

MAKES 12

PREPARATION TIME 1 HOUR

COOKING TIME 15—20 MINUTES

INGREDIENTS

110 g / 4 oz / ⅔ cup self-raising flour, sifted

110 g / 4 oz / ½ cup caster (superfine) sugar

110 g / 4 oz / ½ cup butter, softened

2 large eggs

2 tbsp unsweetened cocoa powder

50 ml / 1 ¾ fl. oz / ¼ cup stout

TO DECORATE

400 ml / 14 fl. oz / 1 ⅔ cups double (heavy) cream

150 g / 5 ½ oz / ⅔ cup green ready-to-roll fondant icing

green sprinkles

METHOD

- Preheat the oven to 190°C (170°C fan) / 375F / gas 5 and line a 12-hole cupcake tin with paper cases.

- Measure the cake ingredients into a bowl then whisk together for 3 minutes or until smooth and light.

- Divide the mixture between the paper cases and bake for 15–20 minutes or until a skewer inserted into the centre comes out clean. Leave to cool completely.

- Whip the cream until it holds its shape, then pipe a swirl on top of each cake.

- Roll out the green fondant and cut out 12 shamrock shapes, then transfer them to the top of the cakes and sprinkle with green hundreds and thousands.

TOP TIP

Add a few drops of green food dye to the cream for novelty value.

134

Blue Baby Feet Cupcakes

MAKES 12

PREPARATION TIME 1 HOUR 10 MINUTES

COOKING TIME 15–20 MINUTES

INGREDIENTS

110 g / 4 oz / ⅔ cup self-raising flour, sifted

110 g / 4 oz / ½ cup caster (superfine) sugar

110 g / 4 oz / ½ cup butter, softened

large eggs

lemon, juiced and zest finely grated

TO DECORATE

400 g / 14 oz / 2 cups ready-to-roll fondant icing

blue and pink food dye

icing (confectioners') sugar for dusting

METHOD

- Preheat the oven to 190°C (170°C fan) / 375F / gas 5 and line a 12-hole cupcake tin with paper cases.

- Combine the flour, sugar, butter, eggs and lemon juice and zest in a bowl and whisk together for 2 minutes or until smooth. Divide the mixture between the cases, then transfer the tin to the oven and bake for 15–20 minutes or until a toothpick inserted into the centre comes out clean.

- Test with a wooden toothpick, if it comes out clean, the cakes are done. Transfer the cakes to a wire rack and leave to cool completely.

- Dye two thirds of the fondant icing blue. Dust the work surface lightly with icing sugar and roll out the blue icing. Use a cookie cutter the same diameter as the top of the cakes to cut out 12 circles then attach them to the top of the cakes with a dab of water.

- Finely chop the remaining white fondant icing and put it in a small bowl. Gradually work in warm water a few drops at a time until you have a thick but pipable icing.

- Add a tiny amount of pink food dye to turn the icing light pink.

- Spoon half of the icing into a piping bag fitted with a flat nozzle and pipe 2 feet onto each cake.

- Use a damp paint brush to tidy up the edges of the icing to give a smooth outline.

- Spoon the rest of the icing into a piping bag fitted with a small plain nozzle and pipe on the toes.

- Use a damp paint brush to flatten down the tops of the icing dots to remove any points.

Egg Basket Cupcakes

MAKES 12

PREPARATION TIME 40 MINUTES

COOKING TIME 15–20 MINUTES

INGREDIENTS

110 g / 4 oz / ⅔ cup self-raising flour, sifted

110 g / 4 oz / ½ cup caster (superfine) sugar

110 g / 4 oz / ½ cup butter, softened

2 large eggs

1 tsp vanilla extract

TO DECORATE

100 g / 3 ½ oz / ½ cup butter, softened

200 g / 7 oz / 2 cups icing (confectioners')
    sugar

1 tbsp unsweetened cocoa powder

72 chocolate mini eggs

METHOD

- Preheat the oven to 190°C (170°C fan) / 375F / gas 5 and line a 12-hole cupcake tin with paper cases.

- Combine the flour, sugar, butter, eggs and vanilla extract in a bowl and whisk together for 2 minutes or until smooth. Divide the mixture between the cases, then transfer the tin to the oven and bake for 15–20 minutes.

- Test with a wooden toothpick inserted into the centre; if it comes out clean, the cakes are done. Transfer the cakes to a wire rack and leave to cool completely.

- Beat the butter until smooth, then add the icing sugar and cocoa powder to the bowl.

- Beat the mixture with a wooden spoon to make a smooth chocolate buttercream.

- Spoon the mixture into a piping bag, fitted with a large basket weave nozzle and pipe an undulating ring of icing on top of each cake.

- Arrange 6 chocolate mini eggs on top of each cake.

TOP TIP

For an extra chocolatey treat, add 2 tbsp of cocoa powder to the cake mixture.

Toasted Marshmallow Cupcakes

MAKES 12

PREPARATION TIME 45 MINUTES

COOKING TIME 15–20 MINUTES

INGREDIENTS

110 g / 4 oz / ⅔ cup self-raising flour, sifted

110 g / 4 oz / ½ cup caster (superfine) sugar

110 g / 4 oz / ½ cup butter, softened

2 large eggs

1 tsp vanilla extract

TO DECORATE

200 g / 7 oz / 2 cups marshmallow fluff

150 g / 5 ½ oz / 2 ½ cups mini marshmallows

METHOD

- Preheat the oven to 190°C (170°C fan) / 375F / gas 5 and line a 12-hole cupcake tin with paper cases.

- Whisk the cake ingredients together for 3 minutes or until smooth. Divide the mixture between the cases and bake for 15–20 minutes.

- Test with a wooden toothpick inserted into the centre; if it comes out clean, the cakes are done. Leave to cool completely.

- Spread the cakes with marshmallow fluff, then pile the mini marshmallows on top.

- Use a blowtorch to toast the top of the marshmallows, then serve straight away.

TOP TIP

If you don't have a blowtorch, toast the tops under a very hot grill.

Chocolate Caramel Curl Cupcakes

MAKES 12

PREPARATION TIME 50 MINUTES

COOKING TIME 10–15 MINUTES

INGREDIENTS

110 g / 4 oz / ⅔ cup self-raising flour, sifted

110 g / 4 oz / ½ cup caster (superfine) sugar

110 g / 4 oz / ½ cup butter, softened

2 large eggs

75 g / 2 ½ oz / ½ cup caramel pieces

TO DECORATE

100 g / 3 ½ oz / ½ cup butter, softened

200 g / 7 oz / 2 cups icing (confectioners') sugar

2 tbsp caramel syrup

2 tbsp unsweetened cocoa powder

4 tbsp white chocolate curls

METHOD

- Preheat the oven to 190°C (170°C fan) / 375F / gas 5 and line a 12-hole cupcake tin with paper cases.

- Combine the flour, sugar, butter, eggs and caramel pieces in a bowl and whisk together for 2 minutes or until smooth.

- Divide the mixture between the cases, then transfer the tin to the oven and bake for 10–15 minutes. Test with a wooden toothpick inserted into the centre; if it comes out clean, the cakes are done. Transfer the cakes to a wire rack and leave to cool completely.

- Beat the butter until smooth, then gradually whisk in the icing sugar and caramel syrup. Spoon the buttercream into a piping bag fitted with a large star nozzle and pipe a big swirl onto each cake. Sprinkle with white chocolate curls to finish.

TOP TIP

For coffee enthusiasts, try adding 1 tsp of espresso powder to the cake mixture.

Trophy Cupcakes

MAKES 12

PREPARATION TIME 1 HOUR

COOKING TIME 15–20 MINUTES

INGREDIENTS

110 g / 4 oz / ⅔ cup self-raising flour, sifted

110 g / 4 oz / ½ cup caster (superfine) sugar

110 g / 4 oz / ½ cup butter, softened

2 large eggs

1 tsp vanilla extract

TO DECORATE

400 ml / 14 fl. oz / 1 ⅔ cups double (heavy) cream

110 g / 4 oz / ⅓ cup ready-to-roll fondant icing

gold food dye spray paint

yellow sugar stars

METHOD

- Preheat the oven to 190°C (170°C fan) / 375F / gas 5 and line a 12-hole cupcake tin with paper cases.

- Measure the cake ingredients into a bowl then whisk together for 3 minutes or until smooth and light.

- Divide the mixture between the paper cases and bake for 15–20 minutes or until a skewer inserted into the centre comes out clean. Leave to cool completely.

- Whip the cream until it holds its shape, then pipe a swirl on top of each cake.

- Shape the fondant icing into 12 trophies and mark a number 1 onto each one. Spray the trophies gold, then transfer them to the top of the cakes and surround with sugar stars.

TOP TIP

You can also cut the fondant icing into round medals with a cookie cutter.

Bonfire Cupcakes

MAKES 12

PREPARATION TIME 30 MINUTES

COOKING TIME 15–18 MINUTES

INGREDIENTS

110 g / 4 oz / ⅔ cup self-raising flour, sifted

110 g / 4 oz / ½ cup margarine, softened

110 g / 4 oz / ½ cup caster (superfine) sugar

1 tsp orange flower water

2 large eggs

a pinch of salt

TO DECORATE

200 g / 7 oz / 1 cup butter, softened

400 g / 14 oz / 4 cups icing (confectioners') sugar

1 tsp orange flower water

a few drops of orange food dye

75 g / 2 ½ oz / ½ cup milk chocolate, chopped

METHOD

- Preheat the oven to 180°C (160°C fan) / 350F / gas 4 and line a 12-hole cupcake tin with 12 cupcake cases.

- Beat together all the ingredients for the batter in a mixing bowl for 2 minutes until smooth and creamy.

- Divide evenly between the paper cases before rapping the tin on a work surface to help settle the batter.

- Bake for 15–18 minutes until risen; test with a wooden toothpick inserted into the centre; if it comes out clean, the cakes are done.

- Transfer the cakes to a wire rack and leave to cool.

- Beat the butter with the icing sugar and orange flower water until smooth.

- Set aside half of the buttercream and spread the rest over the cakes.

- Dye the reserved buttercream orange and pipe a ring of teardrops round the outside of each cake.

- Sprinkle the centres with chopped chocolate.

TOP TIP
Sprinkle the chocolate with red glitter sugar to make it look like glowing embers.

White Almond Cupcakes

MAKES 12

PREPARATION TIME 30 MINUTES

COOKING TIME 15–20 MINUTES

INGREDIENTS

110 g / 4 oz / ⅔ cup self-raising flour, sifted

110 g / 4 oz / ½ cup caster (superfine) sugar

110 g / 4 oz / ½ cup butter, softened

2 large eggs

½ tsp almond essence

TO DECORATE

200 g / 7 oz / ⅔ cup ready-to-roll fondant icing

12 white carnations

METHOD

- Preheat the oven to 190°C (170°C fan) / 375F / gas 5 and line a 12-hole cupcake tin with paper cases.

- Combine the cake ingredients and whisk together for 2 minutes.

- Divide the mixture between the cases and bake for 15–20 minutes or until a toothpick inserted into the centre comes out clean.

- Transfer the cakes to a wire rack and leave to cool.

- Roll out the icing and cut out 12 circles the same size as the cakes using a fluted cutter.

- Wet the backs and stick them to the cakes, then top with the carnations.

TOP TIP

Add 50 g of chopped almonds to the cake mixture for added crunch.

149

Teddy Bear Cupcakes

MAKES 12

PREPARATION TIME 1 HOUR 45 MINUTES

COOKING TIME 15–20 MINUTES

INGREDIENTS

110 g / 4 oz / ⅔ cup self-raising flour, sifted

110 g / 4 oz / ½ cup caster (superfine) sugar

110 g / 4 oz / ½ cup butter, softened

1 tsp vanilla extract

2 large eggs

TO DECORATE

100 g / 3 ½ oz / ½ cup butter, softened

200 g / 7 oz / 2 cups icing (confectioners')
    sugar

1 tsp vanilla extract

450 g / 1 lb / 2 cups brown ready-to-roll
    fondant icing

black food dye pen

white and yellow sugar butterflies

METHOD

- Preheat the oven to 190°C (170°C fan) / 375F / gas 5 and line a 12-hole cupcake tin with paper cases.

- Whisk the cake ingredients together until smooth and light. Divide the mixture between the paper cases and bake for 15–20 minutes or until a toothpick inserted into the centre comes out clean. Leave to cool completely.

- Whisk the buttercream ingredients together for 2 minutes then pipe a swirl on top of each cake.

- Model the brown fondant into 12 teddy bears, attaching the head and limbs with a dab of water. Use a cocktail stick to mark on the seam and add the facial features with the black food dye pen.

- Transfer the teddies to the top of the cakes and surround them with sugar butterflies.

TOP TIP
Add a handful of milk chocolate chips to the cake mixture for a touch of luxury.

Caramel Popcorn Cupcakes

MAKES 12

PREPARATION TIME 55 MINUTES

COOKING TIME 15–20 MINUTES

INGREDIENTS

110 g / 4 oz / ⅔ cup self-raising flour, sifted
110 g / 4 oz / ½ cup caster (superfine) sugar
110 g / 4 oz / ½ cup butter, softened
1 tsp vanilla extract
2 large eggs

TO DECORATE

100 g / 3 ½ oz / ½ cup butter, softened
200 g / 7 oz / 2 cups icing (confectioners')
    sugar
100 g / 3 ½ oz / 4 cups sweet popcorn
110 g / 4 oz / ½ cup granulated sugar

METHOD

- Preheat the oven to 190°C (170°C fan) / 375F / gas 5 and line a 12-hole cupcake tin with paper cases.

- Whisk the cake ingredients together until smooth and light. Divide the mixture between the paper cases and bake for 15–20 minutes or until a toothpick inserted into the centre comes out clean. Leave to cool completely.

- Whisk the butter until smooth, then gradually incorporate the icing sugar and whip for 2 minutes.

- Spoon the buttercream onto the cakes and top with popcorn.

- Heat the granulated sugar in a saucepan over a medium heat until it starts to melt round the edges. Continue to heat without stirring until all of the sugar melts and turns a light caramel dye, swirling the pan occasionally. Drizzle the caramel over the cupcakes and leave to set.

TOP TIP
Try adding 2 tbsp of popcorn syrup to the cake mixture.

Frog Prince Cupcakes

MAKES 12

PREPARATION TIME 1 HOUR 15 MINUTES

COOKING TIME 15–20 MINUTES

INGREDIENTS

110 g / 4 oz / ⅔ cup self-raising flour, sifted

110 g / 4 oz / ½ cup caster (superfine) sugar

110 g / 4 oz / ½ cup butter, softened

2 tbsp unsweetened cocoa powder

a few drops of peppermint essence

2 large eggs

TO DECORATE

1 egg white

200 g / 7 oz / 2 cups icing (confectioners')
    sugar, sieved

a few drops of peppermint essence

450 g / 1 lb / 2 cups ready-to-roll fondant
    icing

green, yellow and metallic gold food dye

12 sugar flowers

METHOD

- Preheat the oven to 190°C (170°C fan) / 375F / gas 5 and line a 12-hole cupcake tin with paper cases.

- Whisk the cake ingredients together then divide between the paper cases and bake for 15–20 minutes or until a toothpick inserted into the centre comes out clean. Leave to cool completely.

- Whisk the egg white until foamy, then whisk in the icing sugar. Add the peppermint essence a few drops at a time until it reaches the consistency of thick double cream. Spread the icing over the cakes.

- Reserve a small piece of fondant for the balls, then dye the rest green and divide into 12 pieces. Shape each piece in a silicone frog mould, then transfer to the cakes and paint on the details with green food dye. Add a sugar flower to each one.

- Dye the reserved fondant yellow and roll into 12 balls, then add to the cakes and paint them gold.

TOP TIP

For a mint chocolate chip alternative, add chocolate chips to the cake mixture.

Tool Time Cupcakes

MAKES 12

PREPARATION TIME 1 HOUR 30 MINUTES

COOKING TIME 15–20 MINUTES

INGREDIENTS

110 g / 4 oz / ⅔ cup self-raising flour, sifted

110 g / 4 oz / ½ cup caster (superfine) sugar

110 g / 4 oz / ½ cup butter, softened

1 tsp vanilla extract

2 large eggs

DECORATE

450 g / 1 lb / 2 cups ready-to-roll fondant icing

brown, red and silver food dye

METHOD

- Preheat the oven to 190°C (170°C fan) / 375F / gas 5 and line a 12-hole cupcake tin with paper cases.

- Whisk the cake ingredients together until smooth then divide between the paper cases and bake for 15–20 minutes.

- Test the cakes with a toothpick inserted into the centre; if it comes out clean, the cakes are done. Leave to cool completely.

- Dye three quarters of the fondant brown then roll it out and cut out 12 circles. Wet the backs and smooth them onto the cakes. Use a sharp knife to mark the centre; floor boards, then mark on the wood grain and nail holes with a toothpick.

- Model the hammer and saw out of the rest of the fondant, then paint them with the food dyes for an authentic look.

TOP TIP

Add 2 tbsp of unsweetened cocoa powder to the cake mixture.

Golf Cupcakes

MAKES 12
PREPARATION TIME 1 HOUR 30 MINUTES
COOKING TIME 15–20 MINUTES

INGREDIENTS

110 g / 4 oz / ⅔ cup self-raising flour, sifted
110 g / 4 oz / ½ cup caster (superfine) sugar
110 g / 4 oz / ½ cup butter, softened
75 g / 2 ½ oz / ⅓ cup sultanas
2 large eggs

TO DECORATE

225 g / 8 lb / 1 cup ready-to-roll fondant icing
green, red and black food dye
12 lollipop sticks

METHOD

- Preheat the oven to 190°C (170°C fan) / 375F / gas 5 and line a 12-hole cupcake tin with paper cases.

- Whisk the cake ingredients together for 3 minutes then divide between the paper cases and bake for 15–20 minutes.

- Test the cakes with a toothpick inserted into the centre; if it comes out clean, the cakes are done. Leave to cool completely.

- Dye three quarters of the icing green then roll it out and cut out 12 circles the same diameter as the top of the cakes. Brush the backs with water and smooth them onto the cakes.

- Dye a third of the remaining fondant black and make into the holes. Attach to the cakes and insert a lollipop stick into each one. Dye another third of the fondant red and shape into the flags, then use the remaining fondant to make the golf balls.

TOP TIP
Replace the sultanas with chopped hazelnuts (cobnuts) for a nutty crunch.

Toffee Flapjack Cupcakes

MAKES 12

PREPARATION TIME 50 MINUTES

COOKING TIME 10–15 MINUTES

INGREDIENTS

110 g / 4 oz / ⅔ cup self-raising flour, sifted
110 g / 4 oz / ½ cup caster (superfine) sugar
110 g / 4 oz / ½ cup butter, softened
2 large eggs
75 g / 2 ½ oz / ½ cup toffee pieces

TO DECORATE

100 g / 3 ½ oz / ½ cup butter, softened
200 g / 7 oz / 2 cups icing (confectioners')
  sugar
2 tbsp toffee syrup
12 small squares toffee flapjack

METHOD

- Preheat the oven to 190°C (170°C fan) / 375F / gas 5 and line a 12-hole cupcake tin with paper cases.

- Combine the flour, sugar, butter, eggs and toffee pieces in a bowl and whisk together for 2 minutes or until smooth.

- Divide the mixture between the cases, then transfer the tin to the oven and bake for 10–15 minutes. Test with a wooden toothpick inserted into the centre; if it comes out clean, the cakes are done. Transfer the cakes to a wire rack and leave to cool completely.

- Beat the butter until smooth, then gradually whisk in the icing sugar and toffee syrup. Spread the buttercream over the cakes and top with the flapjack squares.

TOP TIP
Replace the toffee pieces with fudge pieces for more indulgence.

Lemon Curd Cupcakes

MAKES 12

PREPARATION TIME 40 MINUTES

COOKING TIME 10–15 MINUTES

INGREDIENTS

110 g / 4 oz / 1 cup self-raising flour, sifted

110 g / 4 oz / ½ cup caster (superfine) sugar

110 g / 4 oz / ½ cup butter, softened

2 large eggs

1 lemon, zest finely grated

TO DECORATE

110 g / 4 oz / ½ cup butter, softened

225 g / 8 oz / 2 cups icing (confectioners')
    sugar, plus extra for dusting

1 tbsp lemon juice

100 g / 3 ½ oz / ⅓ cup lemon curd

METHOD

- Preheat the oven to 190°C (170°C fan) / 375F / gas 5 and line a 12-hole cupcake tin with paper cases.

- Combine the flour, sugar, butter, eggs and lemon zest in a bowl and whisk together for 2 minutes or until smooth.

- Divide the mixture between the cake cases then transfer the tin to the oven and bake for 10–15 minutes. Test with a wooden toothpick inserted into the centre; if it comes out clean, the cakes are done. Transfer the cakes to a wire rack and leave to cool completely.

- To make the buttercream, beat the butter until smooth then beat in the icing sugar. Use a whisk to incorporate the lemon juice, then whisk for 2 minutes or until well whipped.

- Spoon the icing into a piping bag fitted with a large star nozzle and pipe a ring on top of each cake. Fill the centres with lemon curd.

TOP TIP
Use any remaining lemon zest and sprinkle on top of the icing.

Special Occasions

Filigree Swirl Cupcakes

MAKES 12

PREPARATION TIME 1 HOUR 10 MINUTES

COOKING TIME 15–20 MINUTES

INGREDIENTS

110 g / 4 oz / ⅔ cup self-raising flour, sifted

110 g / 4 oz / ½ cup caster (superfine) sugar

110 g / 4 oz / ½ cup butter, softened

2 large eggs

1 tsp vanilla extract

TO DECORATE

200 g / 7 oz / 1 cup ready-to-roll fondant icing

purple food dye

METHOD

- Preheat the oven to 190°C (170°C fan) / 375F / gas 5 and line a 12-hole cupcake tin with paper cases.

- Combine the cake ingredients and whisk until smooth.

- Divide the mixture between the cases and bake for 15–20 minutes or until a toothpick inserted into the centre comes out clean.

- Transfer the cakes to a wire rack and leave to cool.

- Reserve a quarter of the fondant icing. Dye the rest purple and roll out. Cut out 12 circles the same diameter as the cupcakes. Wet the backs and attach to the cakes.

- Put the reserved icing in a bowl and add enough warm water to make a pipable icing, then pipe filigree swirls over the surface of the cakes.

TOP TIP

Add some blueberries and the grated zest of an orange to the cake mixture.

Lemon Fondant Cupcakes

MAKES 12

PREPARATION TIME 1 HOUR 20 MINUTES

COOKING TIME 10–15 MINUTES

INGREDIENTS

110 g / 4 oz / ⅔ cup self-raising flour, sifted

110 g / 4 oz / ½ cup caster (superfine) sugar

110 g / 4 oz / ½ cup butter, softened

2 large eggs

1 lemon, zest finely grated

TO DECORATE

3 tbsp lemon curd

200 g / 7 oz ready-to-roll fondant icing

yellow food dye

1–2 tsp lemon juice

150 g / 5 ½ oz / 1 ½ cups icing (confectioners') sugar

12 sugar flowers

METHOD

- Preheat the oven to 190°C (170°C fan) / 375F / gas 5 and line a 12-hole cupcake tin with paper cases.

- Combine the flour, sugar, butter, eggs and lemon zest in a bowl and whisk together for 2 minutes or until smooth. Divide the mixture between the cases, then transfer the tin to the oven and bake for 10–15 minutes or until a toothpick inserted into the centre comes out clean.

- Test with a wooden toothpick, if it comes out clean, the cakes are done. Transfer the cakes to a wire rack and leave to cool completely.

- Dye the fondant icing yellow, then roll it out and cut out 12 circles a little smaller in diameter than the top of the cakes. Spread the cakes with lemon curd, then smooth the icing on top.

- Add a little lemon juice to the icing sugar, a few drops at a time, until it forms a smooth, spreadable icing. Spoon it into a piping bag fitted with a small plain nozzle and pipe your preferred design onto each cake. Attach the sugar flowers with a little more icing.

TOP TIP
Add crystalised ginger pieces to the mixture for a fiery kick.

Orange Swirl Cupcakes

MAKES 12

PREPARATION TIME 30 MINUTES

COOKING TIME 15–20 MINUTES

INGREDIENTS

FOR THE BATTER

110 g / 4 oz / ⅔ cup self-raising flour, sifted

110 g / 4 oz / ½ cup margarine, softened

110 g / 4 oz / ½ cup caster (superfine) sugar

1 tsp orange flower water

2 large eggs

a pinch of salt

TO DECORATE

200 g / 7 oz / 1 cup butter, softened

400 g / 14 oz / 4 cups icing (confectioners')
    sugar

1 tsp orange flower water

a few drops of orange food dye

12 Cape gooseberries (physalis)

1 orange, zest finely pared

METHOD

- Preheat the oven to 190°C (170°C fan) / 375F / gas 5 and line a 12-hole cupcake tin with paper cases.

- Combine the cake ingredients and whisk together until smooth.

- Divide the mixture between the cases and bake for 15–20 minutes or until a toothpick inserted into the centre comes out clean.

- Transfer the cakes to a wire rack and leave to cool.

- Beat the butter with the icing sugar, orange flower water and food dye until smooth.

- Pipe the icing onto the cakes and garnish each one with a Cape gooseberry and a sprinkle of orange zest.

TOP TIP
Add finely grated orange zest to the cake mixture for a subtle tanginess.

Sweeties Cupcakes

MAKES 12

PREPARATION TIME 50 MINUTES

COOKING TIME 15–20 MINUTES

INGREDIENTS

110 g / 4 oz / ⅔ cup self-raising flour, sifted

110 g / 4 oz / ½ cup caster (superfine) sugar

110 g / 4 oz / ½ cup butter, softened

1 tsp vanilla extract

2 large eggs

TO DECORATE

100 g / 3 ½ oz / ½ cup butter, softened

200 g / 7 oz / 2 cups icing (confectioners') sugar

pink food dye

50 g / 1 ¾ oz / ½ cup sugar-coated sweets

METHOD

- Preheat the oven to 190°C (170°C fan) / 375F / gas 5 and line a 12-hole cupcake tin with paper cases.

- Whisk the cake ingredients together until smooth and light. Divide the mixture between the paper cases and bake for 15–20 minutes or until a toothpick inserted into the centre comes out clean. Leave to cool completely.

- Whisk the butter until smooth, then gradually incorporate the icing sugar and whip for 2 minutes.

- Fit a piping bag with a large star nozzle, then paint a few lines of pink food dye down the inside of the bag. Fill the bag with the buttercream, then pipe a big swirl on top of each cake.

- Decorate the cakes with the sugar-coated sweets.

TOP TIP

For vibrant cakes, fold a handful of mixed sweets through the cake mixture too.

Jelly Bean Cupcakes

MAKES 12

PREPARATION TIME 40 MINUTES

COOKING TIME 10–15 MINUTES

INGREDIENTS

110 g / 4 oz / 1 cup self-raising flour, sifted

110 g / 4 oz / ½ cup caster (superfine) sugar

110 g / 4 oz / ½ cup butter, softened

2 large eggs

1 tsp vanilla extract

TO DECORATE

110 g / 4 oz / ½ cup butter, softened

225 g / 8 oz / 2 cups icing (confectioners')
     sugar, plus extra for dusting

2 tbsp milk

1 tsp vanilla extract

150 g / 5 ½ oz / 1 cup jelly beans

METHOD

- Preheat the oven to 190°C (170°C fan) / 375F / gas 5 and line a 12-hole cupcake tin with paper cases.

- Combine the flour, sugar, butter, eggs and vanilla extract in a bowl and whisk together for 2 minutes or until smooth.

- Divide the mixture between the cake cases then transfer the tin to the oven and bake for 10–15 minutes. Test with a wooden toothpick inserted into the centre; if it comes out clean, the cakes are done. Transfer the cakes to a wire rack and leave to cool completely.

- To make the buttercream, beat the butter until smooth then beat in the icing sugar. Use a whisk to incorporate the milk and vanilla extract, then whisk for 2 minutes or until well whipped.

- Spoon the icing into a piping bag fitted with a large plain nozzle and pipe small teardrops to cover the surface of the cakes. Arrange the jelly beans on top.

TOP TIP

Replace the jelly beans with a swirl of strawberry jam for a classic finish.

Irresistible Dark Chocolate Cupcakes

MAKES 12

PREPARATION TIME 30 MINUTES

COOKING TIME 15–18 MINUTES

INGREDIENTS

110 g / 4 oz / ⅔ cup self-raising flour, sifted

110 ml / 4 fl. oz / ½ cup sunflower oil

110 g / 4 oz / ½ cup caster (superfine) sugar

75 g / 3 oz / ½ cup cocoa powder

30 g / 1 oz / 2 tbsp cornflour (cornstarch)

1 tbsp distilled vinegar

2 large eggs

a pinch of salt

TO DECORATE

175 g / 6 oz / ¾ cup unsalted butter, softened

125 g / 4 ½ oz / 1 cup icing (confectioner's) sugar

50 g / 2 oz / ⅓ cup cocoa powder

2 tbsp whole milk

sugar strands

METHOD

- Preheat the oven to 180°C (160°C fan) / 350F / gas 4.

- Line a 12-hole cupcake tin with 12 cupcake cases.

- Beat together all the ingredients for the batter in a mixing bowl for 2 minutes until smooth.

- Divide evenly between the paper cases before rapping the tin on a work surface to help settle the batter.

- Bake for 15–18 minutes until risen; test with a wooden toothpick inserted into the centre; if it comes out clean, the cakes are done.

- Remove to a wire rack to cool as you prepare the buttercream.

- Beat the softened butter with the cocoa powder, icing sugar and milk in a mixing bowl until smooth and creamy.

- Spoon into a piping bag fitted with a large plain nozzle and pipe in mounds on top of the cupcakes.

- Garnish the buttercream with a sprinkle of sugar strands.

TOP TIP

Top each cake with a chocolate truffle for extra decadence.

Coffee Ruffle Cupcakes

MAKES 12

PREPARATION TIME 35 MINUTES

COOKING TIME 15–18 MINUTES

INGREDIENTS

110 g / 4 oz / ⅔ cup self-raising flour, sifted

110 g / 4 oz / ½ cup margarine

110 g / 4 oz / ½ cup caster (superfine) sugar

55 g / 2 oz / ⅓ cup cocoa powder

55 ml / 2 fl. oz / ¼ cup whole milk

2 large eggs

a pinch of salt

TO DECORATE

100 g / 3 ½ oz / ½ cup butter, softened

200 g / 7 oz / 2 cups icing (confectioners') sugar

2 tbsp cocoa powder

1 tsp instant espresso powder

2 tbsp milk

12 chocolate cigarillos

METHOD

- Preheat the oven to 180°C (160°C fan) / 350F / gas 4 and line a 12-hole cupcake tin with 12 cupcake cases.

- Beat together all the ingredients for the batter apart from the milk in a mixing bowl for 2 minutes until smooth and creamy.

- Add the milk and beat again for a further minute.

- Divide evenly between the paper cases before rapping the tin on a work surface to help settle the batter.

- Bake for 15–18 minutes until risen; test with a wooden toothpick inserted into the centre; if it comes out clean, the cakes are done.

- Transfer the cakes to a wire rack and leave to cool.

- Beat the butter with the icing sugar, cocoa, espresso powder and milk until smooth.

- Pipe a ruffle of buttercream onto each cake and top with the chocolate cigarillos.

TOP TIP

Add 1 tsp of instant espresso powder to the cake mixture for extra coffee flavour.

Chocolate Raspberry Cupcakes

MAKES 12

PREPARATION TIME 45 MINUTES

COOKING TIME 15–18 MINUTES

INGREDIENTS

110 g / 4 oz / ⅔ cup self-raising flour, sifted

110 g / 4 oz / ½ cup margarine, softened

110 g / 4 oz / ½ cup caster (superfine) sugar

55 g / 2 oz / ⅓ cup cocoa powder

55 ml / 2 fl. oz / ¼ cup whole milk

2 large eggs

a pinch of salt

TO DECORATE

100 g / 3 ½ oz / ½ cup butter, softened

200 g / 7 oz / 2 cups icing (confectioners') sugar

50 g / 2 oz / ⅓ cup cocoa powder

2 tbsp whole milk

12 raspberries

METHOD

- Preheat the oven to 180°C (160°C fan) / 350F / gas 4 and line a 12-hole cupcake tin with 12 cupcake cases.

- Beat together all the ingredients for the batter apart from the milk in a mixing bowl for 2 minutes until smooth and creamy.

- Add the milk and beat again for a further minute.

- Divide evenly between the paper cases before rapping the tin on a work surface to help settle the batter.

- Bake for 15–18 minutes until risen; test with a wooden toothpick inserted into the centre; if it comes out clean, the cakes are done.

- Remove to a wire rack to cool as you prepare the buttercream.

- Beat the softened butter with the cocoa powder, icing sugar and milk in a mixing bowl until smooth and creamy.

- Spoon into a piping bag fitted with a large plain nozzle and pipe in swirled mounds on top of the cupcakes

- Garnish the top of the buttercream with a raspberry before serving.

TOP TIP

These cakes also look pretty topped with a whole fresh strawberry.

Raspberry Jelly Sweet Cupcakes

MAKES 12

PREPARATION TIME 45 MINUTES

COOKING TIME 15–18 MINUTES

INGREDIENTS

110 g / 4 oz / ⅔ cup self-raising flour, sifted

110 g / 4 oz / ½ cup margarine, softened

110 g / 4 oz / ½ cup caster (superfine) sugar

1 tsp vanilla extract

2 large eggs

a pinch of salt

TO DECORATE

100 g / 3 ½ oz / ½ cup butter, softened

200 g / 7 oz / 2 cups icing (confectioners') sugar

a few drops of red food dye

12 raspberry jelly sweets

METHOD

- Preheat the oven to 180°C (160°C fan) / 350F / gas 4 and line a 12-hole cupcake tin with 12 cupcake cases.

- Beat together all the ingredients for the batter in a mixing bowl for 2 minutes until smooth and creamy.

- Divide evenly between the paper cases.

- Bake for 15–18 minutes until risen and a toothpick inserted into the centre comes out clean.

- Remove to a wire rack to cool.

- Beat the softened butter in a mixing bowl for 3–4 minutes until pale.

- Add the icing sugar and beat well before beating in the food dye until it turns light pink.

- Spread evenly on top of the cupcakes using a small palette knife, reserving about a third of the icing.

- Spoon the remaining icing into a piping bag and pipe a star of icing on top of the icing and garnish with a sweet.

TOP TIP

You can decorate these cakes with any sweets of your choice.

Fruit and Cream Cupcakes

MAKES 12

PREPARATION TIME 30 MINUTES

COOKING TIME 15–18 MINUTES

INGREDIENTS

110 g / 4 oz / ⅔ cup self-raising flour, sifted

110 g / 4 oz / ½ cup margarine

110 g / 4 oz / ½ cup caster (superfine) sugar

1 tsp vanilla extract

2 large eggs, a pinch of salt

TO DECORATE

300 ml / 10 ½ fl. oz / 1 ¼ cups double
   (heavy) cream

1 tsp vanilla extract

12 Cape gooseberries (physallis)

12 raspberries

12 blackcurrants

1 kiwi fruit, cut into 12 pieces

METHOD

- Preheat the oven to 180°C (160°C fan) / 350F / gas 4 and line a 12-hole cupcake tin with 12 cupcake cases.

- Beat together all the ingredients for the batter in a mixing bowl for 2 minutes until smooth and creamy.

- Divide evenly between the paper cases before rapping the tin on a work surface to help settle the batter.

- Bake for 15–18 minutes until risen; test with a wooden toothpick inserted into the centre; if it comes out clean, the cakes are done.

- Transfer the cakes to a wire rack and leave to cool.

- Whip the cream with the vanilla extract until it holds its shape then spread it liberally over the cakes.

- Top the cakes with the fruit and serve straight away.

TOP TIP

Add 2 tbsp of icing sugar to the cream before whipping for a sweeter flavour.

Chocolate Butterfly Cupcakes

MAKES 12

PREPARATION TIME 45 MINUTES

COOKING TIME 15–18 MINUTES

INGREDIENTS

110 g / 4 oz / ⅔ cup self-raising flour, sifted

110 g / 4 oz / ½ cup margarine, softened

110 g / 4 oz / ½ cup caster (superfine) sugar

1 tsp vanilla extract

2 large eggs

a pinch of salt

TO DECORATE

100 g / 3 ½ oz / ½ cup butter, softened

200 g / 7 oz / 2 cups icing (confectioners')
    sugar

50 g / 2 oz / ⅓ cup cocoa powder

2 tbsp whole milk

chocolate or fondant butterflies

METHOD

- Preheat the oven to 180°C (160°C fan) / 350F / gas 4 and line a 12-hole cupcake tin with 12 cupcake cases.

- Beat together all the ingredients for the batter in a mixing bowl for 2 minutes until smooth and creamy.

- Divide evenly between the paper cases before rapping the tin on a work surface to help settle the batter.

- Bake for 15–18 minutes until risen; test with a wooden toothpick inserted into the centre; if it comes out clean, the cakes are done.

- Remove to a wire rack to cool as you prepare the buttercream.

- Beat the softened butter with the cocoa powder, icing sugar and milk in a mixing bowl until smooth and creamy.

- Spoon into a piping bag fitted with a straight-sided nozzle and pipe in round mounds on top of the cupcakes.

- Garnish the buttercream with a chocolate butterfly before serving.

TOP TIP

Try adding the grated zest of an orange to the buttercream.

Lemon Pink Cupcakes

MAKES 12

PREPARATION TIME 1 HOUR 10 MINUTES

COOKING TIME 15–20 MINUTES

INGREDIENTS

110 g / 4 oz / ⅔ cup self-raising flour, sifted

110 g / 4 oz / ½ cup caster (superfine) sugar

110 g / 4 oz / ½ cup butter, softened

2 large eggs

1 lemon, juiced and zest finely grated

TO DECORATE

100 g / 3 ½ oz / ½ cup butter, softened

60 g / 2 oz / ¼ cup icing (confectioners')
    sugar

½ lemon, juiced and zested

110 g / 4 oz fondant icing

Pink food dye

Sugar sprinkles

METHOD

- Preheat the oven to 190°C (170°C fan) / 375F / gas 5 and line a 12-hole cupcake tin with paper cases.

- Combine the flour, sugar, butter, eggs and lemon juice and zest in a bowl and whisk together for 2 minutes or until smooth. Divide the mixture between the cases, then bake for 15–20 minutes or until a toothpick inserted into the centre comes out clean.

- Transfer the cakes to a wire rack and leave to cool completely.

- Beat the butter with the icing sugar, lemon juice and zest.

- Spoon the mixture into a piping bag, fitted with a large star nozzle and pipe a swirl of buttercream on top of each cake.

- Dye the fondant icing pink and roll it out on a work surface that has been lightly dusted with icing sugar.

- Use a small daisy cutter to cut out 12 flowers and attach one to the top of each cake.

- Sprinkle with sugar sprinkles.

TOP TIP

These cakes are also delicious with lime zest in place of the lemon.

189

Lavender Buttercream Cupcakes

MAKES 12

PREPARATION TIME 30 MINUTES

COOKING TIME 15–18 MINUTES

INGREDIENTS

110 g / 4 oz / ⅔ cup self-raising flour, sifted

110 g / 4 oz / ½ cup margarine, softened

110 g / 4 oz / ½ cup caster (superfine) sugar

1 tsp vanilla extract

2 large eggs

a pinch of salt

TO DECORATE

100 g / 3 ½ oz / ½ cup butter, softened

200 g / 7 oz / 2 cups icing (confectioners') sugar

a few drops of purple food dye

5 drops of lavender essence

12 raspberry jelly sweets

METHOD

- Preheat the oven to 180°C (160°C fan) / 350F / gas 4 and line a 12-hole cupcake tin with 12 cupcake cases.

- Beat together all the ingredients for the cake in a mixing bowl for 2 minutes until smooth and creamy.

- Divide evenly between the paper cases before rapping the tin on a work surface to help settle the batter.

- Bake for 15–18 minutes until risen or until a toothpick inserted into the centre comes out clean.

- Remove to a wire rack to cool.

- Beat the softened butter in a mixing bowl for 3–4 minutes until pale.

- Add the icing sugar, lavender essence and drops of food dye until you have an even, purple buttercream.

- Spoon into a piping bag.

- Pipe a rosette swirl in the centre of the cupcakes and surround with piped stars before garnishing with a jelly sweets on top.

TOP TIP

Add a few drops of lavender essential oil in place of the vanilla.

Vanilla Pearl Cupcakes

MAKES 12

PREPARATION TIME 40 MINUTES

COOKING TIME 10–15 MINUTES

INGREDIENTS

110 g / 4 oz / 1 cup self-raising flour, sifted

110 g / 4 oz / ½ cup caster (superfine) sugar

110 g / 4 oz / ½ cup butter, softened

2 large eggs

1 tsp vanilla extract

TO DECORATE

110 g / 4 oz / ½ cup butter, softened

225 g / 8 oz / 2 cups icing (confectioners') sugar, plus extra for dusting

1 tsp vanilla extract

sugar pearls to decorate

METHOD

- Preheat the oven to 190°C (170°C fan) / 375F / gas 5 and line a 12-hole cupcake tin with paper cases.

- Combine the flour, sugar, butter, eggs and vanilla extract in a bowl and whisk together for 2 minutes or until smooth.

- Divide the mixture between the cake cases then transfer the tin to the oven and bake for 10–15 minutes. Test with a wooden toothpick inserted into the centre; if it comes out clean, the cakes are done. Transfer the cakes to a wire rack and leave to cool completely.

- To make the buttercream, beat the butter until smooth then beat in the icing sugar and vanilla extract. Whisk for 2 minutes or until well whipped.

- Spoon the icing into a piping bag fitted with a large star nozzle and pipe small rosettes over the surface of the cakes. Decorate with the sugar pearls.

TOP TIP

Add ground almonds to the cake mixture for a delicate nutty taste.

Jelly Mint Cupcakes

MAKES 12

PREPARATION TIME 30 MINUTES

COOKING TIME 15–18 MINUTES

INGREDIENTS

110 g / 4 oz / ⅔ cup self-raising flour, sifted

110 g / 4 oz / ½ cup margarine, softened

110 g / 4 oz / ½ cup caster (superfine) sugar

1 tsp vanilla extract

2 large eggs

a pinch of salt

TO DECORATE

100 g / 3 ½ oz / ½ cup butter, softened

200 g / 7 oz / 2 cups icing (confectioners') sugar

vanilla extract

½ tsp peppermint extract

a few drops of red food dye

a few drops of green food dye

12 raspberry jelly sweets

METHOD

- Preheat the oven to 190°C (170°C fan) / 375F / gas 5 and line a 12-hole cupcake tin with paper cases.

- Combine the cake ingredients and whisk together for 2 minutes.

- Divide the mixture between the cases and bake for 15–18 minutes.

- Test with a wooden toothpick inserted into the centre; if it comes out clean, the cakes are done.

- Transfer the cakes to a wire rack and leave to cool.

- Beat the butter with the icing sugar, vanilla extract and peppermint extract until smooth then set aside two thirds of the icing.

- Dye the remaining icing pale pink and spread it over the cakes.

- Dye the reserved icing pale green and pipe it in a ruffle on top of the cakes.

- Top each cake with a jelly sweets.

TOP TIP

Replace the vanilla extract with peppermint, for minty freshness.

194

Chocolate Mint Dream Cupcakes

MAKES 12

PREPARATION TIME 40 MINUTES

COOKING TIME 15–18 MINUTES

INGREDIENTS

110 g / 4 oz / ⅔ cup self-raising flour

110 g / 4 oz / ½ cup margarine

110 g / 4 oz / ½ cup caster (superfine) sugar

55 g / 2 oz / ⅓ cup cocoa powder

55 ml / 2 fl. oz / ¼ cup whole milk

2 large eggs, a pinch of salt

TO DECORATE

200 g / 7 oz / 1 cup butter, softened

400 g / 14 oz / 4 cups icing (confectioners')
    sugar

a few drops of peppermint essence

a few drops of green food dye

12 chocolate cigarillos

24 pieces of chocolate

cocoa powder for dusting

METHOD

- Preheat the oven to 180°C (160°C fan) / 350F / gas 4 and line a 12-hole cupcake tin with 12 cupcake cases.

- Beat together all the ingredients for the batter apart from the milk in a mixing bowl for 2 minutes.

- Add the milk and beat again for a further minute.

- Divide evenly between the paper cases before rapping the tin on a work surface to help settle the batter.

- Bake for 15–18 minutes. Test with a wooden toothpick inserted into the centre; if it comes out clean, the cakes are done.

- Transfer the cakes to a wire rack and leave to cool.

- Beat the butter with the icing sugar, peppermint essence and food dye until smooth then pipe it onto the cakes.

- Top each cake with a cigarillo, 2 pieces of chocolate and a dusting of cocoa.

TOP TIP

Add orange zest to the buttercream instead of peppermint essence.

Flower Basket Cupcakes

MAKES 12

PREPARATION TIME 1 HOUR 45 MINUTES

COOKING TIME 15–20 MINUTES

INGREDIENTS

110 g / 4 oz / ⅔ cup self-raising flour, sifted

110 g / 4 oz / ½ cup caster (superfine) sugar

110 g / 4 oz / ½ cup butter, softened

1 tbsp rose water

2 large eggs

TO DECORATE

100 g / 3 ½ oz / ½ cup butter, softened

200 g / 7 oz / 2 cups icing (confectioners') sugar

1 tsp orange flower water

450 g / 1 lb / 2 cups ready-to-roll fondant icing

brown, purple, yellow and pink food dye

12 tiny sugar butterflies

METHOD

- Preheat the oven to 190°C (170°C fan) / 375F / gas 5 and line a 12-hole cupcake tin with paper cases.

- Whisk the cake ingredients together until smooth then divide the mixture between the paper cases and bake for 15–20 minutes or until a toothpick inserted into the centre comes out clean. Leave to cool completely.

- Whisk the buttercream ingredients together for 2 minutes then spread it onto the cakes.

- Dye two thirds of the fondant brown and roll it out. Cut it into 5 mm / ¼ in strips, then weave them into a lattice and transfer to the top of the cakes. Twist the remaining strips to form the basket handles.

- Divide up the remaining fondant and dye it different pastel shades. Roll them out and use a small blossom plunger cutter to cut out the flowers and place them straight onto the cakes.

- Add a butterfly to each one.

TOP TIP

Try adding lavender essential oil to the buttercream.

Mint Truffle Cupcakes

MAKES 12

PREPARATION TIME 30 MINUTES

COOKING TIME 15–18 MINUTES

INGREDIENTS

110 g / 4 oz / ⅔ cup self-raising flour, sifted

110 g / 4 oz / ½ cup margarine

110 g / 4 oz / ½ cup caster (superfine) sugar

1 tsp vanilla extract

2 large eggs, a pinch of salt

TO DECORATE

200 g / 7 oz / 1 cup butter, softened

400 g / 14 oz / 4 cups icing (confectioners') sugar

a few drops of peppermint essence

2 tbsp cocoa powder

2 tbsp milk

a few drops of green food dye

12 chocolate drops

multi-dyeed sugar strands

METHOD

- Preheat the oven to 180°C (160°C fan) / 350F / gas 4 and line a 12-hole cupcake tin with 12 cupcake cases.

- Beat together all the ingredients for the batter.

- Divide evenly between the paper cases.

- Bake for 15–18 minutes. Test with a wooden toothpick inserted into the centre; if it comes out clean, the cakes are done.

- Transfer the cakes to a wire rack and leave to cool.

- Beat the butter with the icing sugar and peppermint essence until smooth.

- Set aside a third of the buttercream and whisk the cocoa and milk into the rest.

- Pipe a swirl of cocoa buttercream onto each cake.

- Dye the reserved icing green and pipe it on top then garnish with chocolate drops and sugar strands.

TOP TIP

Try adding green food dye to the cake mixture.

Pearls Cupcakes

MAKES 12

PREPARATION TIME 1 HOUR 30 MINUTES

COOKING TIME 15—20 MINUTES

INGREDIENTS

110 g / 4 oz / ⅔ cup self-raising flour, sifted

110 g / 4 oz / ½ cup caster (superfine) sugar

110 g / 4 oz / ½ cup butter, softened

2 large eggs

1 lemon, juiced and zest finely grated

TO DECORATE

400 g / 14 oz / 1 cup ready-to-roll fondant
    icing

ivory food dye

icing (confectioners') sugar for dusting

pearlescent dusting powder

METHOD

- Preheat the oven to 190°C (170°C fan) /
  375F / gas 5. Line a cupcake tin with
  12 paper cases.

- Combine the flour, sugar, butter, eggs
  and lemon juice and zest and whisk for
  2 minutes. Divide between the cases,
  then bake for 15–20 minutes or until a
  toothpick inserted into the centre comes
  out clean. Leave to cool.

- Dust a surface with icing sugar and roll
  out two thirds of the fondant icing. Use a
  scalloped edge cutter to cut out 12 circles.

- Attach one circle to the top of each cake
  with water and reserve the off-cuts.

- Dye the rest of the icing ivory and roll it
  out. Use a smaller scalloped edge cutter to
  cut out 12 circles and attach each one to
  the top of a cake.

- Roll the white icing off-cuts into a 5 mm
  (¼ in) diameter sausage and cut into 5 mm
  (¼ in) lengths. Roll each piece into a ball
  and coat in pearlescent powder.

- Brush the rim of the ivory icing circles
  with water. Place pearls where the icing is
  wet. Add a pearl to the centre of each cake.

TOP TIP

Replace the lemon with
the juice and zest of
two limes.

Indigo Sugar Cupcakes

MAKES 12

PREPARATION TIME 45 MINUTES

COOKING TIME 15–18 MINUTES

INGREDIENTS

FOR THE BATTER

110 g / 4 oz / ⅔ cup self-raising flour, sifted

110 g / 4 oz / ½ cup margarine, softened

110 g / 4 oz / ½ cup caster (superfine) sugar

1 tsp vanilla extract

2 large eggs

a pinch of salt

TO DECORATE

225 g / 8 oz / 1 cup unsalted butter, softened

400 g / 14 oz / 4 cups icing (confectioners')
    sugar

1 tbsp lemon juice

a few drops of purple food dye

2 tbsp purple sugar sprinkles

METHOD

- Preheat the oven to 180°C (160°C fan) / 350F / gas 4 and line a 12-hole cupcake tin with 12 cupcake cases.

- Beat together all the ingredients for the batter in a mixing bowl for 2 minutes until smooth and creamy.

- Divide evenly between the paper cases before rapping the tin on a work surface to help settle the batter.

- Bake for 15–18 minutes until risen or until a toothpick inserted into the centre comes out clean.

- Remove to a wire rack to cool.

- Beat the butter with the icing sugar, lemon juice and drops of food dye until you have an even light purple butter.

- Spread the tops of the cupcake evenly with half of the purple buttercream before spooning the remainder into a piping bag fitted with a small star-shaped nozzle.

- Pipe stars of buttercream around the perimeter of the cupcakes before sprinkling the centres with sugar.

TOP TIP
Add a handful of fresh blackcurrants through the cake mixture when in season.

Strawberry Sweeties Cupcakes

MAKES 12

PREPARATION TIME 1 HOUR

COOKING TIME 15–20 MINUTES

INGREDIENTS

110 g / 4 oz / ⅔ cup self-raising flour, sifted

110 g / 4 oz / ½ cup caster (superfine) sugar

110 g / 4 oz / ½ cup butter, softened

2 large eggs

1 tsp vanilla extract

TO DECORATE

100 g / 3 ½ oz / ½ cup butter, softened

200 g / 7 oz / 2 cups icing (confectioners') sugar

½ tsp vanilla extract

12 packets of violets sweets

36 strawberry jelly sweets

METHOD

- Preheat the oven to 190°C (170°C fan) / 375F / gas 5 and line a 12-hole cupcake tin with paper cases.

- Combine the flour, sugar, butter, eggs and vanilla extract and whisk together for 2 minutes. Divide the mixture between the cases, then transfer the tin to the oven and bake for 15–20 minutes or until a toothpick inserted into the centre comes out clean.

- Transfer the cakes to a wire rack and leave to cool.

- Beat the butter until smooth, then gradually whisk in the icing sugar and vanilla extract.

- Spoon the mixture into a piping bag, fitted with a large star nozzle and use two thirds of the buttercream to pipe a rosette on top of each cake.

- Open the packets of violets sweets and press them round the outside of the buttercream rosette.

- Pipe the remaining buttercream into a rosette on top of each cake.

- Top each cake with 3 strawberry jelly sweets.

TOP TIP

You can decorate these cakes with sweets of your choice.

Jelly Bean Cream Cupcakes

MAKES 12

PREPARATION TIME 45 MINUTES

COOKING TIME 10–15 MINUTES

INGREDIENTS

110 g / 4 oz / ⅔ cup self-raising flour, sifted

110 g / 4 oz / ½ cup caster (superfine) sugar

110 g / 4 oz / ½ cup butter, softened

1 tsp vanilla extract

2 large eggs

TO DECORATE

400 ml / 14 fl. oz / 1 ⅔ cups double (heavy) cream

150 g / 5 ½ oz / 1 cup jelly beans

METHOD

- Preheat the oven to 190°C (170°C fan) / 375F / gas 5 and line a 12-hole cupcake tin with paper cases.

- Measure the cake ingredients into a bowl then whisk together for 3 minutes or until smooth and light. Divide the mixture between the paper cases, then transfer the tin to the oven and bake for 10–15 minutes.

- Test the cakes with a toothpick inserted into the centre; if it comes out clean, the cakes are done. Transfer the cakes to a wire rack and leave to cool completely.

- Whip the cream until it holds its shape, then spread it onto the cakes and decorate with the jelly beans.

TOP TIP

Replace the jelly beans with real orange and pineapple pieces for fruity goodness.

White-choc Heart Cupcakes

MAKES 12

PREPARATION TIME 1 HOUR

COOKING TIME 15–20 MINUTES

INGREDIENTS

110 g / 4 oz / ⅔ cup self-raising flour, sifted

110 g / 4 oz / ½ cup caster (superfine) sugar

110 g / 4 oz / ½ cup butter, softened

2 large eggs

75 g / 2 ½ oz / ½ cup white chocolate chips

TO DECORATE

100 g / 3 ½ oz / ½ cup butter, softened

200 g / 7 oz / 2 cups icing (confectioners') sugar

1 tsp vanilla extract

72 white chocolate hearts

12 chocolate cigarillos

METHOD

- Preheat the oven to 190°C (170°C fan) / 375F / gas 5 and line a 12-hole cupcake tin with paper cases.

- Whisk the cake ingredients together for 3 minutes or until smooth. Divide the mixture between the cases and bake for 15–20 minutes.

- Test with a wooden toothpick inserted into the centre; if it comes out clean, the cakes are done. Leave to cool completely.

- Beat the butter until smooth, then gradually whisk in the icing sugar and vanilla extract.

- Spoon the buttercream into a piping bag fitted with a large star nozzle and pipe a big swirl onto the cupcakes.

- Top each cake with 6 white chocolate hearts and a cigarillo.

TOP TIP
Add 1 tsp of vanilla extract to the cake mixture for a sweeter flavour.

Coconut Star Cupcakes

MAKES 12

PREPARATION TIME 1 HOUR

COOKING TIME 15–20 MINUTES

INGREDIENTS

110 g / 4 oz / ⅔ cup self-raising flour, sifted

110 g / 4 oz / ½ cup caster (superfine) sugar

110 g / 4 oz / ½ cup butter, softened

3 tbsp desiccated coconut

2 tbsp milk

2 large eggs

TO DECORATE

100 g / 3 ½ oz / ½ cup butter, softened

200 g / 7 oz / 2 cups icing (confectioners')
    sugar

50 g / 1 ¾ oz / ½ cup desiccated coconut

150 g / 5 ½ oz / ⅔ cup blue ready-to-roll
    fondant icing

METHOD

- Preheat the oven to 190°C (170°C
  fan) / 375F / gas 5 and line a 12-hole
  cupcake tin with paper cases.

- Measure the cake ingredients into
  a bowl then whisk together for 3
  minutes or until smooth and light.
  Divide the mixture between the
  paper cases, then transfer the tin to
  the oven and bake for 15–20 minutes.

- Test the cakes with a toothpick
  inserted into the centre; if it comes
  out clean, the cakes are done. Leave
  to cool completely.

- Whisk the butter until smooth, then
  gradually incorporate the icing sugar
  and coconut and whisk until smooth.
  Pipe a big swirl onto each cake.

- Roll out the blue fondant and cut out
  12 large stars, using the offcuts to
  make the smaller stars. Transfer to
  the top of the cakes.

TOP TIP

Top the cakes with
shredded coconut
before adding
the stars.

Silver Sprinkle Cupcakes

MAKES 12

PREPARATION TIME 40 MINUTES

COOKING TIME 10–15 MINUTES

INGREDIENTS

110 g / 4 oz / 1 cup self-raising flour, sifted

110 g / 4 oz / ½ cup caster (superfine) sugar

110 g / 4 oz / ½ cup butter, softened

2 large eggs

1 tsp vanilla extract

TO DECORATE

110 g / 4 oz / ½ cup butter, softened

225 g / 8 oz / 2 cups icing (confectioners')
    sugar, plus extra for dusting

1 tsp vanilla extract

silver sugar sprinkles to decorate

METHOD

- Preheat the oven to 190°C (170°C fan) / 375F / gas 5 and line a 12-hole cupcake tin with paper cases.

- Combine the flour, sugar, butter, eggs and vanilla extract in a bowl and whisk together for 2 minutes or until smooth.

- Divide the mixture between the cake cases then transfer the tin to the oven and bake for 10–15 minutes. Test with a wooden toothpick inserted into the centre; if it comes out clean, the cakes are done. Transfer the cakes to a wire rack and leave to cool completely.

- To make the buttercream, beat the butter until smooth then beat in the icing sugar and vanilla extract. Whisk for 2 minutes or until well whipped.

- Spoon the icing into a piping bag fitted with a large star nozzle and pipe it onto the cakes. Finish with a scattering of silver sprinkles.

TOP TIP

Add chocolate chips to the cake mixture for a sweeter treat.

Coffee Truffle Cupcakes

MAKES 12

PREPARATION TIME 45 MINUTES

COOKING TIME 15–18 MINUTES

INGREDIENTS

110 g / 4 oz / ⅔ cup self-raising flour, sifted

110 g / 4 oz / ½ cup margarine

110 g / 4 oz / ½ cup caster (superfine) sugar

55 g / 2 oz / ⅓ cup cocoa powder

55 ml / 2 fl. oz / ¼ cup whole milk

2 large eggs, a pinch of salt

TO DECORATE

100 g / 3 ½ oz / ½ cup butter, softened

200 g / 7 oz / 2 cups icing (confectioners')
  sugar

50 g / 2 oz / ⅓ cup cocoa powder

2 tbsp whole milk

1 tsp strong instant espresso powder

1 tsp pink sugar pearls

1 tsp white sugar pearls

METHOD

- Preheat the oven to 180°C (160°C fan) / 350F / gas 4 and line a 12-hole cupcake tin with 12 cupcake cases.

- Beat together all the ingredients for the batter apart from the milk in a mixing bowl for 2 minutes.

- Add the milk and beat again for a further minute.

- Divide evenly between the paper cases before rapping the tin on a work surface to help settle the batter.

- Bake for 15–18 minutes until risen or until a toothpick inserted into the centre comes out clean.

- Remove to a wire rack to cool.

- Beat the softened butter with the cocoa powder, icing sugar and milk in a mixing bowl until smooth.

- Mix together the espresso powder with 1 tbsp boiling water until smooth, then beat into the buttercream.

- Spoon into a piping bag fitted with a star-shaped nozzle and pipe a swirled mound on top of each cupcake.

- Garnish the buttercream with a few sugar pearls.

TOP TIP
These cakes also look great topped with chocolate coated coffee beans.

Broderie Anglaise Cupcakes

MAKES 12

PREPARATION TIME 1 HOUR 15 MINUTES

COOKING TIME 15–20 MINUTES

INGREDIENTS

110 g / 4 oz / ⅔ cup self-raising flour, sifted

110 g / 4 oz / ½ cup caster (superfine) sugar

110 g / 4 oz / ½ cup butter, softened

1 tbsp rose water

2 large eggs

TO DECORATE

1 egg white

200 g / 7 oz / 2 cups icing (confectioners')
    sugar, sieved

a few drops of rose water

pink food dye

225 g / 8 oz / 1 cup ready-to-roll fondant icing

METHOD

- Preheat the oven to 190°C (170°C
  fan) / 375F / gas 5 and line a 12-hole
  cupcake tin with paper cases.

- Whisk the cake ingredients together
  until smooth then divide between
  the paper cases and bake for 15–20
  minutes or until a skewer inserted
  into the centre comes out clean.
  Leave to cool completely.

- Whisk the egg white until foamy,
  then add the icing sugar and whip for
  3 minutes. Add the rose water a few
  drops at a time until it reaches the
  consistency of thick double cream.

- Reserve a little of the icing for piping
  and dye the rest pink. Spread it over
  the cakes.

- Roll out the fondant and use a lace
  or Broderie anglaise cutter to cut out
  the flower ribbons, attaching them
  with a dab of water.

- Use the reserved white icing to pipe
  on the rest of the details.

TOP TIP

Try a pale blue dye in
place of the pink for a
different look.

INDEX